W9-BIQ-462

PORTFOLIO DEVELOPMENT AND ADULT LEARNING
Purposes and Strategies

PORTFOLIO DEVELOPMENT AND ADULT LEARNING
Purposes and Strategies

Alan Mandell and Elana Michelson
with contributions from 15 leading experts in the field.

Property of
FAMILY OF FAITH
LIBRARY

© 1990, CAEL.

All rights reserved. Except for the inclusion of brief quotations in a review in a magazine, journal or newspaper, no part of this book may be reproduced or utilized in any form or by any means, electronic or mechanical, including photo-copying, recording or by any information storage and retrieval system, without permission in writing from the publisher.

ISBN: 0-9628073-0-3

CAEL
The Council for Adult and Experiential Learning
223 West Jackson, Suite 510
Chicago, Illinois 60606

Faculty of Pratt Library

CONTENTS

Contents

This book fills a major gap in the literature about adult students returning to college. As portfolio-assisted prior learning assessment has become recognized as an important service, the available literature has focused on helping students navigate the process and on helping institutions ensure both quality and accessibility. There is a further need, however, for those students and institutions to understand adults' claims to prior learning and current competence as integral parts of their reentry into collegiate studies.

Neither in CAEL publications nor elsewhere, to the best of my knowledge, is there a thorough treatment that responds to that need. Adults' educational goals and career development choices may well be most helpfully approached through a process which integrates an inventory of their prior learning, clarification of their life aspirations, and a sound exploration for themselves of their academic skills. The plans for college study thereby generated, however, must also fit within the curricular options permitted by the particular college or university.

In Part 1 of this volume, the authors lay out a schematic for faculty deliberations on these issues. Eight alternative rationales are spelled out to illustrate the potential for portfolio development courses which are responsive to the particular institution's philosophy, to the students being served, and to the career or disciplinary focus of the students' proposed studies. Each rationale posits a particular approach to portfolio development curriculum and includes purposes, strategies, and specific curricular suggestions.

A specific college rarely adopts a portfolio development program for a single purpose. The actual courses through which students write their portfolios and design their degrees, therefore, rarely fit theoretical models exactly. For this reason, the editors have invited some twelve colleges with substantial experience in portfolio-assisted assessment and collegiate re-entry to describe their programs and explain their rationales and operations. Notes between these case studies offer analytic and comparative perspective. Thus a practitioner can see how the abstract themes identified in Part 1 may be combined in actual course plans which reflect multiple purposes.

Learning portfolios are more than simply instruments to facilitate sound assessment. They are themselves vehicles to facilitate further learning. The primary value of the assessment experience is rarely the academic credit awarded for a successful claim to knowledge and competence: it is more likely to be a learner's clearer awareness of his or her own potential. Insight on one's potential may lead to a change in educational and career plans, or to the learner's grasp for the first time of key values and priorities of a liberal education. This understanding may in turn save many worried days of confusion and may help the faculty member engage the learner's own commitment to the institution's aspirations for the program.

The process of development learning portfolios offers ways of going at the questions of re-entry adults in an appropriate order and at appropriate times. Ideally all prospective college students would have thought through these issues of their potential, their aspirations, and the best arena and means for pursuing them, at least in broad outline, before choosing a college and entering it. For most learners an in-depth exploration of the issues needs the help of processional practitioners, and that help may first be available, as the practical cases depicted here indicate, shortly after admission, but at the very beginning of formal studies. Others make better use of the opportunity if it occurs later in the collegiate experience (see the College of New Rochelle report, for example) or intermittently over a longer period of time (see the Alverno study). As you read this book, think of it, not as a set of ideal models, but as a working tool for helping you think through your own best ideas for launching returning adults into their undergraduate studies.

Not all of the practitioners using this book may be as concerned with the theory underlying alternative uses of portfolios as they are with the problems of selecting and implementing their own particular approach to portfolio development. Such practitioners may wish to skip the theoretical introduction and only skim Part 1 for general themes and possibilities. The introduction to Part 2 will allow those focused exclusively on practice to make good use of the case descriptions presented there.

As readers reflect upon the theory of portfolio development laid out in Part 1 of this book and the variety of implementations exhibited in Part 2, they will see that the strategy of portfolio development is one that can benefit learners of all ages and interests; and the forms which portfolios can take are legion. May this book serve, then, to stimulate its users to go beyond the practices here described to tailor their own programs in creative ways to fit their distinctive circumstances and their diverse learners.

Morris T. Keeton
Senior Fellow, CAEL
March 1990

ACKNOWLEDGMENTS

This book grew out of the faculty development efforts of the College and University Options Program of UAW-Ford. In seeking to prepare faculty and college administrators to address the needs of auto workers, the United Auto Workers and Ford Motor Company provided us with the occasion not only to serve a new population of adult students but to rethink many issues in adult higher education as a whole. Our thanks go first to our CAEL associates who, under the leadership of Pam Tate, worked on that ground-breaking project.

Many people helped to mold this book into its present form. The inclusion of actual working models of portfolio development was central to our purpose, and our gratitude goes to the authors of the chapters in Part 2 for their contribution. Working with them has consistently been a pleasure, both because of their innovative models of portfolio development and because of their willingness to bear with us, to rewrite paragraphs just one more time, to help us mold the chapters into a whole. At various stages along the way, Lois Lamdin graciously lent us her encouragement and her fine reader's eye and, with Urban Whitaker and Marty Thorsland, ensured that we included perspectives that would otherwise have been missed. Above all, Morris Keeton nurtured and guided this project from its inception. His vision of adult education has inspired us, as it has many others; his support and careful attention to details made this publication possible.

The ideas in this book, like most ideas, evolved experientially, in this case in the day-to-day life of Empire State College. Our understanding has grown through interaction with colleagues and friends who approach education with both rigor and passion—and with the freedom to experiment that Empire State provides. Our deepest thanks go to our students, who have taught us more about the meaning and ownership of knowledge than we could ever have hoped to learn.

Alan Mandell
Elana Michelson
New York City
March 1990

INTRODUCTION

The introduction of prior learning assessment has been one of the most significant recent breakthroughs in higher education. We have come to recognize that students, particularly adult learners, enter our institutions with rich clusters of college-level knowledge and skill gained from myriad sources. Acknowledging the educational validity of students' prior learning and translating that learning into college credit has both righted the traditional injustice against individuals whose education has taken place outside the academy and enriched the academy itself. In institutionalizing prior learning assessment, colleges and universities have given new life to the interaction among cultures of knowledge and informed our understanding of the relationship between learning and practical activity.

Yet beneath a well-earned pride in our new policies and practices lie deeper questions and important philosophical issues that hold no ready answers. We have had to respond to the particular configurations of academic strengths and weaknesses that adults often bring with them when they return to school. We have been pushed to articulate, question, and remold the way we define and evaluate knowledge. We have had to step back and examine our tacit understandings of what constitutes a college education and its role in this society. And we have had to wonder, perhaps more fundamentally than ever, about the level, relevance, and structuring of the body of knowledge that we want our students to master. In many exciting and demanding ways, the practice of prior learning assessment and the diverse clientele of adult students it serves have provided a critical occasion to reflect on what we do and why we do it.

One significant area of reflection concerns our basic definition of academic knowledge and its relationship to the learning gained through work and community involvement. How, for example, do we remain sufficiently attentive to the contours and limitations of our own habits of academic thought, with their emphasis on theoretical knowledge divided conveniently into disciplines? Can we encourage a receptivity to the academic credibility of learning that does not follow the conventional patterns or that reflects a distinctive confluence of theory, practice, and historical development? How do we respond to and quantify knowledge that does not fit our categories without undercutting or distorting the significance of that knowledge to a person's life?

These issues are not unrelated to the fact that the assessment of prior learning explicitly encourages a nontraditional population to enter higher education. Thus, other difficult questions emerge as well. To what extent, for example, do our unexamined assumptions about people's age, gender, class, and racial background influence our attitudes, not only about what they are *capable* of learning but about what they have already learned? Do the narrative styles they use to present their knowledge influence our assessment of the knowledge itself? How do we ensure that our judgments are not class-specific, not bounded by vocabularies that we hold sacred but that may be of only limited applicability when listening to another quality of experience?

Finally, we are pushed to examine the relationship between where students have been and where they are going and between what they know and what they will learn in college. As many of the approaches in this book make clear, the assessment of students' prior learning provides a vital opportunity for educational and career planning and for the identification of students' interests, aspirations, and strengths.

To help our students engage in that exploration, we must bring into focus our own assumptions and ideals about the autonomy of the adult learner and about the parameters of individual choice. How can we ensure that our guidance is as student oriented as possible, offering the widest field of choice and opportunity that our specific institution allows? How can we encourage students to become responsible for their educational choices, calling on the best of self-determined and self-empowered adult higher education while simultaneously providing a background for informed educational planning?

As with our definitions of knowledge and our assumptions about age, gender, class, and race, this issue is not without its broader social components. As our students often know better than we do, individual educational planning is done within the context of other planning that has already taken place. How do we provide information and insight into this "preplanning:" corporate plans for technological change and the restructuring of the workforce, for example, or public policy decisions about the relationship between education and employment? Do we hold our own ideas about what constitutes a "good" plan or an informed decision? How do we make explicit our own judgments and help our students to critique their own?

The answers we explicitly or implicitly posit to these philosophical speculations have specific ramifications for the practice of prior learning assessment within our institutions. Many colleges, for instance, allow prior learning to be assessed on solely a course-specific or department-specific basis: thus, students' knowledge can be accredited only to the degree that it dovetails with the divisions of knowledge specific to a particular institution. This policy, which makes sense within certain university contexts, works against students with job-based knowledge, the categories of which are often only accidentally aligned with academic departments and courses. In other cases, institutions permit assessment of more eclectic configurations of learning, but demand that the students themselves relate their knowledge to certain theoretical and self-reflective norms of academia. Again, that policy may be academically justifiable, but it can leave students out in the cold.

In all cases, the central piece of prior learning assessment is the portfolio development course, for it is here that both the challenges of prior learning assessment and their resolutions converge. The context in which our students articulate their knowledge and request that it be translated into college credit is the nexus where student and institution meet and in which we become the translators, so to speak, among varied cultures of knowledge. How we help our students negotiate the adjustment to academic ways of seeing and view their knowledge both in its own and in academic terms can mean the difference between success and failure both for our students and for our institutions' ability to serve them.

The eight approaches to portfolio development courses that make up Part 1 of this volume were designed to support that difficult negotiation. By exploring the worlds of work and community as well as the mores and codes of academia, the approaches focus attention on the points at which old and new learning meet. Far from being purely speculative, however, the eight approaches introduce activities that are the stuff of daily life in institutions across the United States. The models that make up Part 2 were chosen for their success in bringing cultures of knowledge together and for their commitment to providing a space for that encounter.

PART 1
Approaches

INTRODUCTION TO PART 1

The learning that students bring with them from previous collegiate and noncollegiate study, from the workplace, and from organizational and community life is at the heart of the curriculum of any portfolio development course. Those experiences must be articulated and documented, organized into disciplines and interdisciplinary categories, and evaluated by teams of appropriate experts from the faculty. However we structure it, much of the work of a portfolio development course is therefore procedural: the how-to's of assessment; the formatting of portfolios; and the long process of documenting and evaluating knowledge. Yet the narrative itself, and the portfolio development course in which it is written, represent the student's single most significant opportunity to reflect on the role of education in his or her life and to examine prior learning within the new context of academic modes of knowledge.

While practices vary somewhat among institutions, all procedures for quality portfolio-assisted assessment have similar requirements. Portfolios must be structured in such a way as to go far beyond a narrative of experiences; students must distinguish between learning and experience, articulate their knowledge and its utilization, and establish interconnections between theory and practice in their field. The writing and documenting of an extended portfolio narrative is thus a challenging task for most students, and one that requires the active participation of faculty.

That is not to say that the portfolio narrative is the only acceptable framework for the assessment of prior learning. In some situations, case studies, product and performance demonstrations, standardized exams, and other alternative methods provide a basis for evaluation that is both fairer to students and more responsive to the field itself. Thus, students in the theoretical and applied sciences may be better served by nationally standardized exams—in organic chemistry, for example, or in any defined undergraduate study in which a nationally uniform curriculum is maintained. Similarly, students in artistic, technical, and other primarily nonverbal fields are often at a disadvantage when their ability to verbalize their skills becomes a more central criterion than the skills themselves—studio art or programming in COBOL, for instance, are best assessed by evaluating the art or the programs themselves.

Even in cases where it does not serve as the primary method of assessment, however, the portfolio narrative adds an important reflective dimension to the assessment process. First, the narrative requires that the students themselves examine the nature and form of their prior education. Second, it ensures that students not only receive credit for college-level prior learning but also consider its connections to academic modes of thought.

This reflective dimension is valuable even in cases in which student's prior knowledge is not creditable as college-level learning. In cases of paraprofessional work, for example, the nature and structure of a student's knowledge may lack the systematic theoretical framework required of academic learning. Yet the student's workplace history may still have fostered important analytical and decision-making skills. The opportunity to reflect on and articulate the successful acquisition of skills in the past can build confidence and pride even when it does not lead to a credit award.[1]

The completion of the portfolio narrative itself can thus be of major benefit to students. The course within which portfolio development takes place, however, has important benefits of its own. In addition to examining prior learning, such a course requires that students look beyond their own histories and explore the relationship of the self to social institutions and the stages of human development. Through readings, writing assignments, research projects, and class activities, students are encouraged to make connections among the worlds of work, schooling, family, and community and to acquire new communication and analytical skills.

Thus, the course gives students opportunities to view their prior learning from various perspectives and within new contexts. At the same time, it requires new learning in the humanities, social sciences, and communication arts. The worlds of work and learning, the foundations of personal growth and employment satisfaction, the philosophy of education, and the development of academic skills all provide filters through which portfolio development courses can be structured as significant educational experience.

It is for this reason that many colleges give credit for the portfolio development course. To receive credit for the course itself, as opposed to credit for prior learning, students must demonstrate that they have acquired new academic knowledge and skills. Principles of good practice

---

[1]*Research has shown that students often complete the experience with increased self-confidence, greater ability to organize information, and a clearer sense of academic and personal goals. See, for example, J.R. Warren, and P.W. Breen,* The Educational Value of Portfolio and Learning Contract Development *(Columbia, MD.: CAEL), 4–6.*

3

distinguish between noncredit-bearing courses focusing exclusively on portfolio development and credit-bearing courses that offer new synthesis and new learning.

This text introduces eight approaches to portfolio development courses, eight orientations toward integrating prior learning assessment with broadly based learning projects and goals. The eight approaches are less separate curricular outlines, however, than they are emphases within a single intellectual exploration, clusters of interrelated concerns around which appropriate subject matter can be organized. While each approach can and does stand on its own, none is meant to be pursued in isolation from the others. There are obvious points of overlap among the eight orientations, topics form continuities from theme to theme, and individual activities and assignments will work within many approaches.

The Approaches

The first two approaches, "Academic Skills" and "College Orientation," acquaint students with the academic tools that will be relevant to their future fields of study. The two provide a practical introduction to the academic terrain of college study. A third approach, "Personal Exploration," helps students think about their past and future through the lens of their own development as learners, workers, and family members. Such an autobiographical orientation gives students an opportunity to see how their own process of self-assessment and self-reflection can initiate questions about personal and professional goals.

Another theme around which courses can be organized is education itself. This fourth approach uses "The Meaning of Education" to survey the ways in which philosophers from different times and cultures have grappled with the very definition of knowledge. Students are thus provided with a fuller context of interpretation within which to think about the value of their own knowledge and their own experience of schooling.

The next three approaches use work as the focus of the portfolio development course. In the "Careers" orientation students can research the competencies demanded in their career choices or more systematically examine career options as well as their own needs and goals. For those students who have already chosen a course of study, "Introduction to a Field" focuses the portfolio development course on students' particular Academic, Professional, or Technical field of choice. Such an approach allows students to examine and order their past knowledge in the context of an overview of their field as an academic subject and to begin developing an historical or theoretical perspective.

"The Experience of Work" encourages students to examine the wider circumstances, issues, and problems that have influenced their work lives and to situate their own experience within the social organization of work. Both approaches provide students with a significant opportunity to connect their education with their work in both its practical dimension and its broader social and historical context.

The final approach described in this manual is called "Degree Design." This focus is useful in those academic settings where assessment does not exist within pre-defined curricula and where students have wide opportunities to design individual programs. Here, students can use the portfolio development course to explore their individual learning goals and to investigate the ways in which the ideas, methods, and questions of any number of academic fields can help them to develop a personal approach to their college studies. Thematic and interdisciplinary approaches can be investigated using many of the topics, assignments, and concerns of the previous approaches described here.

Criteria for Selection

Choosing among the approaches presented here can be difficult, especially for institutions, faculty members, and academic counselors who are new to portfolio development. Using the approaches eclectically to evolve one's own curriculum can be even more confusing. The criteria for decision making are therefore important to understand. While the weight given to each varies from situation to situation, the applicability of the various approaches depends on three interrelated factors: student needs, faculty expertise and interest, and institutional demands.

Student Needs

Choices concerning the appropriateness of specific approaches must take into account both the level of academic skills and the prior learning typical of students in a specific course. Students with substantial creditable expertise but weak "academic" skills, for example, may find it helpful to focus on the relationships among different kinds of knowledge. The instructor may therefore wish to adapt the "Academic Skills" approach to examine such issues as transferable skills, academic skill development, and the relationship between workplace and college expertise. More generally, the academic level at which students enter the course is a crucial factor in designing an appropriate curriculum: the course can be a major help to students in bridging the academic gap, or it can confirm their worst fears about their capacities for college study.

A second factor in this regard is the orientation of the students toward vocational or personal development. What they need from the portfolio development course, in other words, is in part determined by what they want from their education. Courses for students with highly focused career ambitions, for example, may productively expose those students to the importance of the liberal arts—arguably, in fact, they should—but curriculum must be structured around a respect for and recognition of students' own aspirations and goals.

Finally, attention should be paid to students' cultural orientation and relationships to cultural norms. Such factors as gender, for example, have often created a cultural inclination for or against public self-exploration and self-assessment, and no approach can succeed whose major orientation creates a high degree of discomfort among students. Students' relationship to the majority culture is similarly important. Their sense of access to or alienation from the arts and liberal studies is likely to be mediated by issues of race, ethnicity, gender, and class. Their sense of academic and intellectual discourse may well depend on its historical use within their community as a tool of their own empowerment or a weapon used against them.

Faculty Expertise and Interest

Assignment to a portfolio development course often presents faculty members and counselors with the challenge of professional development. Such courses expose us to different social institutions, populations, life experiences, and fields of inquiry, all of which require new types of understandings and skills. The fostering of prior learning assessment through the UAW-Ford College and University Options Program, for example, brought many academics to a new understanding of life on an assembly line, the impact of changing technology, and the reality of threatened job loss and social displacement.

Even without the challenge of teaching portfolio development courses, the assessment process requires interaction among faculty. Principles of good assessment practice mandate that faculty assess only that knowledge that falls within their expertise; the interdisciplinary nature of much experiential learning thus requires the interaction of faculty experts from a variety of fields. Assessing the college-level experiential learning of a personnel manager, for example, may bring together faculty assessors from the business, psychology, and labor relations departments. Assessing a supervising dietician may require dialog between health sciences and the human resource management faculty. Aside from the benefits to students and the important issues of academic quality control, this interaction can be stimulating for faculty members in separate and isolated departments whose fields of inquiry reflect on each other in the practical activity of the nonacademic world.

Still, our choices among approaches to portfolio development courses must take into account our own current strengths and our willingness to develop new expertise. Nurse's aides, for instance, might profit greatly from a holistic exposure to the biological sciences, the history of medicine, the history of women's work and traditional women's lore, and the career options within the nursing profession. Not all college counselors and faculty members have expertise in any of these areas, however, and few have expertise in them all. Thus, our wish to respond to our students' needs must be tempered by a realistic evaluation of our ability to do justice to various approaches and/or our institutions' openness to team teaching and interdisciplinary study.

Institutional Demands

Finally, the placement of prior learning assessment within the structure of our institutions can be critical in weighing our options for effective portfolio development courses. The policy that determines *when* in a student's education assessment takes place, for example, can be decisive: institutions that place assessment in the early semesters encourage a "College Orientation" approach, whereas institutions requiring that several semesters transpire before students register for the course imply a more retrospective, analytical examination. Other factors such as the length of the course, the size and composition of the group, the credit or noncredit status of the course, and the placement of the course within a specific academic or student service department render various approaches more or less applicable. Equally significant are the assessment methodologies permitted by institutional policy and the evaluation of prior learning on a course-specific or noncourse-specific basis.

To a certain extent, the approaches presented here have been structured with these policy variables in mind. In some cases, the approaches closely parallel academic and student service departments in which portfolio development courses are frequently lodged: the "Academic Skills" approach may be most natural within the English or academic skills department, "Personal Exploration" within the psychology or counseling department, "The Meaning of Education" within the education department, and "Careers" within the career counseling department. In other cases, however, the match between institutional policies and appropriate approaches is more amorphous. The requirement of course-specific assessment, for instance, almost mandates that the course address academic divisions of knowledge, and the requirement of a detailed portfolio narrative demands that a good deal of time be devoted to self-assessment and communication skills. Here, as with the evaluation of student needs, we are obligated to be fair to our students, to use the course to facilitate a successful melding of prior learning and current academic requirements and a meaningful negotiation of what can be a time-consuming and confusing assessment process.

The eight approaches presented here, then, are simply places to start; they must be tailored to the needs of particular institutions, student populations, faculty interests, and academic/professional areas. They are meant to be picked apart and recombined, amended and supplemented by newly developed materials, and improved upon continually. It is in beginning to see the possibilities for portfolio development courses and their intimate connections to issues of real academic relevance that these suggestions are introduced and explored.

ACADEMIC SKILLS

A. Introduction

Adults who are returning to school or entering college for the first time often come with strengths in one area and obvious weaknesses in another. Some, for example, can write with comfort and clarity but have little experience with graphs and statistics. Others can communicate information but have never been asked to develop an argument or to critique a piece of writing. Adults' skills are thus quite often unevenly developed or could use refreshing and practice.

For almost all of our students, the portfolio development course offers opportunities to work on and view the necessity of a broad range of academic skills. These skills can include remediation and introductory work in writing, reading, math, and vocabulary building. In addition, students can be helped to examine the way they reason and analyze. The "Academic Skills" approach give students the chance to practice communication and analytical skills in the context of prior learning; rather than critiquing and writing about unfamiliar and alien subject matter, they can grapple with and communicate knowledge in their own fields of expertise, over which they have mastery of valuable information and sophisticated ideas. Finally, this approach is a forum for familiarizing students with the academic conventions for reasoning and analyzing that may differ from analytical systems they employ competently and appropriately in other contexts.

Compiling a portfolio using this approach allows students to think about their skills in fuller terms, identify academically transferable skills they already possess, become aware of skills they could develop through their college studies, and gain some initial practice in some of those skills. In this sense, the skills approach provides a strong bridge between present skills and future choices of study. Helping students to define their strengths and weaknesses can also facilitate a concrete assessment of their learning needs and educational goals.

B. When to Use This Approach

This approach is of obvious advantage for students who need to practice specific academic skills. Students can identify academic weaknesses in the context of other areas of real strength and can be given regular and sustained assistance in articulating what they know in written form.

This approach works best when

- students in the workshop have rather homogeneous levels of academic skill;

- the workshop instructor is an experienced teacher of writing and academic skills or an academic adept at writing across the curriculum;

- the assessment process occurs at the early stages of a student's college career; and

- the development of an extended portfolio narrative is an expected outcome of the workshop.

C. Sample Topics to Be Covered

1. The meaning and practice of critical thinking and academic skills.

2. The development of skills through experience.

3. The assessment of communication, quantitative, and analytical skills.

4. The development of reading and analytical skills, especially as appropriate to portfolio development: making a deduction, drawing a conclusion, applying theory, making a choice.

5. The development of writing skills, especially as appropriate to portfolio development: overcoming writing block, articulating information, providing examples, describing a process, editing, writing multiple drafts.

D. Sample Assignments and Activities

1. Using the portfolio narrative as the major writing assignment, work with individual students, small groups, and the class on writing, detailing, revising, and organizing written work.

2. Ask students to write an autobiography as a portfolio writing or early draft activity, stressing the usefulness of free writing and

early drafts as ways to discover ideas, generate material for writing, and overcome writing anxiety.

3. Using sections of the developing portfolios as the major writing assignment, give students practice in various rhetorical forms: narration, description, categorization, argumentation, comparison/contrast, process.

4. Over a period of weeks, allow the class or small groups to share their portfolio narratives-in-progress. After listening to individuals read their drafts, ask the rest of the group to discuss what is strong and clear in what they have heard and what is unclear. The class is thus encouraged to learn from one another while providing each other feedback for subsequent drafts.

5. Through class discussion, identify the range of "academic skills" (comprehension, critical thinking, writing and computational skills); work with students to identify the academically transferable skills they have developed through their work and community lives. Urban Whitaker and Paul Breen, *Bridging the Gap: A Learner's Guide to Transferable Skills* is a good workbook for this exercise.

6. Assign readings in areas in which students have significant experiential learning. These readings can be fictional or biographical narratives or discussions of job-related phenomena and social trends. Ask students to compare and contrast the information conveyed with the knowledge they have gained through their own experience.

7. Select and assign two readings in areas in which students have significant experiential learning and in which the authors analyze the same issues but reach different conclusions. Through class discussion and small group work, ask students to critique the evidence and arguments, using their experience and knowledge to evaluate the merits of each position.

8. Assign a short article on a central phenomenon, concern, or issue of common interest to students in the class. Ask students to create a list of key ideas in the article. Discuss with the class the basis for their lists and the general criteria for identifying important points and main ideas in their reading.

9. Ask students to use their experience as well as their writing and analytical skills to evaluate a problem in their work or community activity, analyze why the problem occurs, suggest possible solutions, and explain why the proposed solutions would work. Possible topics include job productivity and satisfaction, strains in

contemporary family life, crime in modern society, interpersonal relations, and women's work experience.

10. Through assignments, exams, and counseling, evaluate students' strengths and weaknesses in skills areas. Work with the class to identify the skills necessary for successful college work and help each student to plan compensatory course work that will enable him or her to gain those skills and fulfill college requirements.

11. Practice oral communication skills and encourage pride and confidence by asking several students at each class session to give a brief lesson in a branch of their experiential learning. Encourage discussion to help students compare their own experiences with those of their classmates and to think about the reasons for similarities and/or differences.

12. Teach library and research skills by familiarizing students with the journals and other library resources in their areas of work and community expertise.

13. Help students think about the meaning of academic skills by looking at a topic such as "literacy" or "the educated person." Ask students to locate materials that could help them to think about their definitions and work with them to pinpoint some of the conflicts of interpretation regarding the terms themselves. Books such as Jonathan Kozol, *Prisoners of Silence*; Paulo Freire, *Education for Critical Consciousness*; E. D. Hirsch, *Cultural Literacy*; C. A. Bowers, *Cultural Literacy for Freedom*; and Sylvia Ashton-Warner, *Teacher* may be good starting points for faculty or students.

14. Ask students to collect current newspaper or journal articles that use graphs, statistics, or numerical data. Use discussion of these materials to identify the use of quantitative methods both in research and analysis and in everyday understanding of things.

E. Case Study: Piotr Cherlianis

Piotr Cherlianis works as a Senior Clerk in the Motor Vehicles Bureau. As the grandson of immigrants in a tightly knit ethnic community, he is active in cultural affairs. He came back to school after his union negotiated a promotion for anyone earning an associate's degree.

Piotr has some office and organizational skills and wishes to major in office management. In addition, he has extensive knowledge of his ethnic language and culture. He has done almost no writing since graduating from high school, however, and needs a great deal of work in that area, not only in grammar but also in the structure and development of written communications.

For Piotr, as for many adult students, a major component of the work he must do in college revolves around academic skills. Work in this area is both the key to his advancement and his key stumbling block. Creating a portfolio can give him an appropriate way to practice communication skills, both in the writing itself and in analyzing and discussing related readings.

Part of Piotr's written work in the course, of course, must be done in his essays applying for prior learning credit; his knowledge of language and culture may well be creditworthy, although secretarial expertise (and what is thought of as "women's work" in general) tends to be underassessed. A substantial portion of his written work, however, can focus on assignments that will help him bridge the gap between his current skills and future academic activity.

As a narrative based on personal experience, the portfolio itself is an appropriate exercise for beginning the "Academic Skills" course. It is more than a personal narrative: to articulate what he knows, Piotr must analyze the flow of work in his office, the categories of activity and knowledge present on the job site, and his own role within the process. Experience with paraprofessional workers suggests that this can be a substantive and important assignment. While workers may be weak in "academic" analytical skills and have trouble interpreting written material, they have highly sophisticated job-based analytical skills. In Piotr's case, assignments focusing on the social relationships, productivity patterns, and organizational structure of the workplace can foster communication skills in a complex area that is already part of his expertise. Similarly, he can practice reading skills through articles on office work, state service, and office technology. Exercises comparing and contrasting the readings with Piotr's own experience on the job can play an important role. The "Academic Skills" approach in this case provides a real transition, not only between two disparate kinds of skills but within a continuum of knowledge that includes both academic and experiential learning.

COLLEGE ORIENTATION

A. Introduction

Adult students have often gained substantive knowledge and sophisticated skills through noncollegiate experiences but have had little or no opportunity to work in a formal college setting. Much about this new world may be alien and forbidding: not only understanding the structure of a college, the vocabulary of the academic world, and the definition of academic disciplines but writing a research paper, taking notes, or finding one's way around a college library.

For students who are new to the academic world, the portfolio development workshop is an appropriate "College Orientation." In this approach, for example, the student can be introduced to a new vocabulary of academic terms as well as to some of the more practical methods of reading a text, writing a research paper, budgeting study-time, or taking a test.

An interesting variation on this model is the use of a student's area of expertise as the take-off point for learning about the definitions of specific academic disciplines. Becoming more aware of the different approaches to their own areas of prior expertise can help students to understand the perspectives of various disciplines and their approach to a topic or a problem.

Compiling a portfolio using these kinds of activities allows students to gain immediate and practical knowledge of the skills and routines that college study will demand and to translate their knowledge into the categories of academic disciplines. It can also help them become more aware of both the areas of knowledge they have already mastered and those that will demand more attention in the future. These activities can also help acquaint them with the specific academic requirements of the college and the program of study they plan to pursue.

B. When to Use This Approach

"The College Orientation" approach has the advantage of easing students' introduction to an unfamiliar college environment by placing that environment in the context of their previous accomplishments and successes. Assignments focus on familiar areas and problems, and workshop design emphasizes real concerns faced by new students. In addition, the group approach gives individual adults support where they often feel self-conscious about their relative ignorance.

This approach works best when

- the topics chosen and issues explored are concrete;
- the assessment process occurs at the early stages of a student's college career;
- students bring to the workshop an adequate level of communication and analytical skills; and
- workshop instructors can call upon colleagues outside their own departments for cooperation and help in specific areas.

C. Sample Topics to Be Covered

1. The value of experiential learning.

2. The similarities and differences between experiential and formal academic learning.

3. The vocabulary of academia.

4. The history, meaning, and scope of academic disciplines and interdisciplines.

5. College survival skills:
   - Using the library.
   - Reading academic materials.
   - Taking notes.
   - Preparing for an examination.
   - Doing research.
   - Writing and documenting a research paper.
   - Presenting an argument.
   - Creating a time and place for regular study.
   - Managing time.

D. Sample Assignments and Activities

1. Ask students to identify two of their major learning experiences, one in which the learning was in a formal setting and one in which the learning was unstructured and fully experiential. Ask them to relate

- what was learned;
- how it was learned;
- the ways in which the two learning experiences were similar;
- the ways in which the two learning experiences were different; and
- the advantages and disadvantages of each method.

Use the assignment to help students reconsider learning experiences they took for granted and think about the significance of other experiences they had perhaps not considered to be sources of learning.

2. Using the college catalog, ask students to identify a course whose content they believe they have mastered experientially. Then ask them to do one or more of the following:

- obtain a copy of the syllabus, reading list, and requirements;
- review the textbook;
- audit a session of the class;
- interview the professor; and
- interview a student in the class.

Use the assignment to establish how students' knowledge relates to knowledge as organized and transmitted in college courses. (In those institutions awarding credit for prior learning on a course-equivalent basis, this assignment pertains directly to the compiling of the portfolio.)

3. Through a library orientation tour and follow-up assignments, ask students to identify books and articles on an area of their expertise. Use these materials to introduce students to the use of bibliographic data, to familiarize them with tables of contents and indices, and to practice reading comprehension skills and/or academic writing. Among many useful tools are Jacques Barzun and Henry Graff, The *New Researcher*; David Beasley, *How to Use a Research Library*; Thomas Mann, *A Guide to Library Research Methods*; and William Rivers and Susan L. Harrington, *Finding Facts: Research Writing across the Curriculum*.

Portfolio development &
adult learning: purposes
and strategies
LC 5201 .M36 1990

4. ... al phenomenon, concern, or issue ... ily lives. Introduce the academic ... oring how various disciplines and ... ese areas and what questions or ... practitioners. For example, auto ... ics of pricing a car, the industrial ... e, the sociological impact of auto ... eaning of auto parts in contempo- ... This can be done through readings, ... ofessionals in each field, and library ...

5. Ask students to keep a record of unfamiliar or difficult words they come across in the above research. Use these glossaries as a way to build an academic vocabulary and identify the focal concerns of each discipline. Through group discussion, survey key terms, their significance, their assumptions, and their histories.

6. Use students' explorations of their current lives as a means of addressing time management issues that surface for adults returning to school. Assign and guide students through timeline and time-restructuring exercises, using one of the recognized books in the field, such as Alan Lakein, *How to Get Control of Your Time and Your Life*. It may be advisable here to discuss the *different* ways in which students think about their time and the problems of negotiating their distinct responsibilities and priorities.

7. Give students a learning-styles profile exercise. Use the results to help students think about and evaluate their own styles and to become more attentive to the different styles with which they and others feel comfortable. David A. Kolb's *The Learning Styles Inventory* is a useful resource here.

8. Ask students to read and view a series of works of literature and art on a topic of common interest. Appropriate topics vary, but assignments might include short stories and poems, a visit to an art museum, and a cinema or theater trip. Use the assignments as the basis for discussing the ways in which artists and writers see the world and the ways in which the humanities help broaden our understanding of ourselves, one another, and the world.

9. Assign more academically prepared students a book such as Thomas Kuhn, *The Structure of Scientific Revolutions*; Richard Morris, *Dismantling the Universe: The Nature of Scientific Discovery*; or McCain and Segal, *The Game of Science*. All of these

deal with the ways in which scientists have defined problems, moved toward solutions, or changed their ways of thinking. Use the texts as a basis for discussing the general issues of naming a problem, searching for perspectives, and changing our perceptions of the world. Max Weber's classic essay, "Science as a Vocation," provides a basis for a similar inquiry. Assignments for more introductory students might include Lewis Thomas, *Lives of a Cell*, or readings from the works of Loren Eisley or Carl Sagan.

10. Hold a symposium on a given issue, asking various students to represent different disciplines and their points of view. Depending on the liveliness and imaginativeness of the class, you may wish to include costumes symbolizing the various disciplines or ask students to represent actual characters from intellectual history. It may also be appropriate to invite other members of the college or community to attend.

E. Case Study: Mary Roberts

Mary Roberts was born in a small farming community in the South. She came north in the early 1960s and has worked as a therapist's aide in a psychiatric hospital for twenty-five years. While she has had little opportunity for promotion because of her lack of formal education, Mary has been given a great deal of responsibility within her job. She has worked with clients, taught basic life skills to retarded adults, and served in the nutrition and pharmacy departments of the hospital.

Mary has returned to school out of a desire for greater challenges at work and a higher standard of living. She is interested in staying within the same general field but moving up into higher positions. She knows that she is smart, but feels inadequate in making academic and career decisions because, she says, "All I know is my job."

The "College Orientation" approach is an appropriate focus for Mary. Because the vocabulary and institutional practices of academia are new to her,she will find the stress on college survival skills helpful. Even more important will be the use of her experience as a mental healthcare worker to facilitate her introduction to academic disciplines. She can examine differing schools of psychology as a way of understanding both the importance of theory in general and the tools for distinguishing among modes of thought. She can gain exposure to historical, sociological, biological, and ethical studies by reading such works as Paul Starr, *The Social Transformation of American Medicine* or Barbara Ehrenreich and Deidra English, *Witches, Midwives, and Nurses: The*

History of Women Healers. Similarly, she can begin to understand the role of the humanities by examining Ken Kesey, *One Flew Over the Cuckoo's Nest*; Peter Weiss, *Marat/Sade*; or the movie versions of these works. A library assignment can help her develop a bibliography of her own.

The point here is not to limit Mary's studies to ideas and works related to psychology; the "Introduction to a Field" approach, discussed later, differs from "College Orientation" in the specificity of its preprofessional focus. The point, rather, is to help her achieve an understanding of the variety of academic disciplines, the distinct points of reference and emphasis among them, and their collective role in understanding the nature of human life. Mary's experience provides not the point of focus but rather the point of departure toward this academic overview.

Mary can, however, use her broadened understanding of the field of psychology and its professional and institutional structure to begin exploring her own career options. Understanding the differing schools of psychology, the social organization of treatment for the mentally ill and mentally handicapped, and the ethical dimensions of various kinds of work within the field will allow her scope to think about her own career possibilities.

Finally, the "College Orientation" approach asks that Mary write her portfolio in the context of a developing perspective. She will thus come out of the process understanding not only the substantial knowledge and skill she already has but also the relationship of her current knowledge both to the field of psychology and to the range of disciplines.

PERSONAL EXPLORATION

A. Introduction

Many adults decide to return to school at critical junctures in their lives. These points may be ones of conflict and tension or of anticipation and exciting transition, but it is *change* that often defines those moments of college entrance. And change typically brings with it a new self-awareness, an interest in reflecting on one's past and wondering about possible futures.

These students can use the portfolio development workshop as an opportunity to explore their own development as learners, parents, and workers in greater depth. They can use their own lives as the focal point of a self-reflective process that will help them gain a clearer and more meaningful appreciation of what they have done, where they are now, and how they might mold their lives from now on. Or they can use the opportunity to learn about the biographies of others whose lives have followed patterns similar to their own. Here, too, ethnic and gender studies may help students think about the factors that have influenced their lives and that have pushed them in particular directions or led them to a certain social status or employment position.

Compiling a portfolio using this approach allows students to work with various components of their own lives and the life histories that they bring to college. It also provides opportunities for students to explore their interests, more clearly articulate their personal and professional goals, and integrate their work and family lives with their experiences as lifelong learners.

B. When to Use This Approach

This approach allows questions to be asked and issues addressed that are immediately connected to students' own lives. It encourages students to compare their experiences with those of others, which often helps to dispel the kind of isolation that some adult students feel.

This approach works best when

- the personal experiences and concerns of the students are linked to their return to school;
- the world of the "personal" is linked to broader academic disciplines such as women's studies, human development, gerontology, and social history; and
- the instructor is attuned to and provides resources for those students who find the autobiographical focus inappropriate.

C. Sample Topics to Be Covered

1. Life as a source of learning.

2. Similarities and differences between experience and academic knowledge.

3. Biography and autobiography.

4. Self-exploration and goal searching.

5. Stages of human development.

6. Women's experiences, men's experiences, and the ethnic experience.

D. Sample Assignments and Activities

1. Ask students to write about significant experiences in their lives and what they learned from them. Use these descriptions in class discussions as a way to discuss what learning is, examine the connections and differences between experience and academic learning, and help people become more aware of the similarities and differences between key experiences (or themes or problems) in their lives and those of others.

2. Have students choose an autobiography of a person whose life in some way relates to their own. Ask them to read it with an eye to thinking about how that person's life evolved and the social, political, cultural, and personal factors that influenced that life. Alternatively, ask the entire group to read one autobiography—Maxine Hong Kingston, *The Woman Warrior*; *The Autobiography of Malcolm X*; or Richard Rodriguez, *Hunger of Memory*—that focuses on race and ethnicity in the development of the self.

3. Assign a reading that examines life transitions in a theoretical context. Examples are Gail Sheehy, *Passages*; Daniel Levinson,

The Seasons of a Man's Life; Eric Erikson, *Identity and the Life Cycle*; Carol Gilligan, *In a Different Voice*; or essays such as Arthur Chickering and Robert Havighurst, "The Life Cycle" (in Chickering, *The Modern American College*.) It may be important to point out to students that theories are based on underlying values and assumptions. You may, for instance, ask students to keep journals connecting these more theoretical models with their own experiences. Alternately, you may wish to examine how these theories do or do not conform to life events imposed from without, as with an individual in a "settling down" life stage who faces the sudden closing of the facility where he or she works.

4. Use the theme of *change* or *development* as a focus in the course. Assign readings and exercises to help students think about changes in self and society, the interactions between them, and the ways they effect one another.

5. Where the course has been organized along the lines of a certain discipline or population, readings can be assigned as appropriate. For example, a class oriented toward women and women's studies might read materials on the sociology of family, the psychology of women, or women's social roles and status. Alternately, a class of retired persons might work with materials dealing with the politics, economics, and psychology of aging. In effect, various themes can serve as contexts for students to think about the broader terrains of their own search and personal assessment.

6. Assign students one of a variety of fantasy-autobiographies in which they are asked to imagine possible lives. You might ask students to write about their lives "as if" they were preparing the assignment in the year 2000; "as if" they were writing about someone who had already achieved the goals they were setting for themselves; or "as if" they had been born of the opposite sex.

7. Ask students to write about some of the ways in which their lives have been interconnected with the life of their community, that is, how their most personal choices and decisions and ways of life were influenced by the cultures within which they have lived. Descriptive case studies such as J. Anthony Lukas, *Common Ground: A Turbulent Decade in the Lives of Three American Families*, or Frances Fitzgerald, *Cities on a Hill*, can serve as important comparative materials. For a lively, more anthropological approach, you may wish to utilize Marvin Harris, *Why Nothing Works*.

E. Case Study: Joanna Smith

In many ways Joanna Smith fits the traditional image of the adult student: female, middle-aged, middle-class, returning to school out of no financial pressure but with a great need to develop new aspects of selfhood. Joanna received a secretarial diploma in high school and went to work as a legal secretary. She quit work when she married one of the lawyers in the firm. While raising her three children, she did volunteer work with the Girl Scouts, served as an officer in the PTA, and taught Sunday school. Joanna's youngest child has just gone away to college, and Joanna is facing the "empty nest" syndrome.

Joanna has gone back to college out of a general need to structure her time, but she doesn't really believe she is "college material." She also feels, as she puts it, "like the old lady among the college kids." She has no idea of what she wants to study, only a vague sense of having missed out on a great deal, and is afraid that perhaps it is too late.

The "Personal Exploration" approach can give Joanna the three things she needs most: a sense of comfort as an adult learner, an opportunity to view her life dynamically, and a chance to explore goals and interests. Beginning with readings on life transitions and adult development can help to ground Joanna in an organic sense of the stages of her own life and of human life in general and in the sense that she is not alone. Other readings in adult education can help her to see learning as a lifelong process and herself as an active learner and participant in the world. In the context of these readings, Joanna's portfolio can become an opportunity to see how much in her life she has accomplished, how she has always been a worker, doer, and learner even when she was not working for a wage.

Readings in women's studies can buttress this approach in several ways. First, they can help her understand how society undervalues volunteer labor while simultaneously relying on the talents and dedication of the women who do it. Second, they can help her gain perspective on her fears as a woman who is growing older and is no longer defined by a child-nurturing role. Finally, like the readings in adult development and life stages, readings in women's studies can alleviate her sense of isolation by allowing her to see herself as one of many people confronting problems and challenges within the same nexus of societal and personal relationships.

Finally, Joanna has the opportunity to use a life transition to define new ambitions and goals. She doesn't have to work for a salary, but at this stage in her life she may very well wish to do so. Alternately, she may discover new areas of activity and intellectual development. An in-depth exploration of her values and interests may move her beyond her lack of specific goals and help her to structure a fully relevant, self-directed education.

THE MEANING OF EDUCATION

A. Introduction

Part of the challenge of working with adults is helping them to gain familiarity and confidence in a new learning environment. While the experience of learning is not new—adults learn in many ways and in many different contexts—confronting education as a formal and self-conscious activity may be difficult. The transition process can be aided when the portfolio development course is used as an opportunity to explore how learning has been defined and how various educational institutions have organized knowledge in different historical and cultural periods.

Through portfolio development students can become aware of what philosophers and educators have said about the meaning of knowledge and how societies and institutions have structured learning in a variety of ways. In this approach students can examine their own assumptions about learning and their preconceived ideas and values regarding how it is acquired and evaluated by others. Looking at the history of education, the debates over the functions of schools in America, or theories of learning, for example, can also help to familiarize students with key academic terms and help them realize that education is itself open to interpretation and subject to change.

Compiling a portfolio using this approach allows students to reflect on their own learning and schooling experiences within a clearer philosophical and historical context. Students can find new ways to think about the significance of their own learning and about the relationship between what they know, how they learned it, and how that learning is valued (or not valued) in society.

B. When to Use This Approach

This approach helps to introduce the theory, philosophy, and history of education in a way that is personally accessible to students. They are encouraged to reflect on their own educational experiences, but with a new distance encouraged by the readings and other assignments developed by the instructor.

This approach works best when

- issues of value judgments, unexamined assumptions, and received ideas are explicitly addressed, worked with, and seen to be open to change;

- abstract concepts are carefully connected to lived experiences; and

- instructors are sufficiently aware of their own value judgments and attitudes so as to be able to present different perspectives and varied interpretations.

C. Sample Topics to Be Covered

1. Philosophies of education from the ancients to the present.

2. Methods for identifying and evaluating skills and technical learning.

3. The history of American schooling.

4. The growth of adult education programs in America.

5. Learning in non-Western societies.

6. The ways specific forms and qualities of knowledge come to be accepted and valued in a society.

7. The meaning of objectivity, truth, and relativity.

8. The differences among going to school as a child, an adolescent, and an adult.

D. Sample Assignments and Activities

1. Ask students to read various essays by educational theorists and philosophers about the topic, What is education? After discussing the ideas and the value judgments contained in these texts, ask students to comment on the ideas, trying to link their own experiences of learning with the authors' perspectives. Key texts in education theory might include Plato's *Republic*, John Dewey, *Experience and Education*, Paulo Freire, *Education for a Critical Consciousness*, and Maxine Greene, *The Dialectic of Freedom*.

2. Have students write autobiographically about their schooling experiences. Discuss these descriptions in class, focusing on the ways

in which these experiences have influenced students' thinking about themselves as learners and their attitudes about a variety of topics, such as authority, discipline, competition, and independence. This kind of exercise can serve as a take-off point for research on connections among students' own experiences and those of other class members, other social groups, members of the opposite gender, and people of other historical periods.

3. Ask students to think about the ways in which the experience of learning as an adult differs from that of children and adolescents. Help them to see how the disadvantages of adult learners (greater responsibilities, less time, etc.) are counterbalanced by adults' greater strengths (clearer motivation, better skills, broader experience, more freedom of choice, etc.). Interested students will find a helpful introduction in Malcolm Knowles, *The Adult Learner: A Neglected Species*. More sophisticated students may be challenged by Stephen Brookfield's *Understanding and Facilitating Adult Learning*.

4. Examine a key debate in the history of American education in the last decades: curriculum, busing, community control, the high dropout rate in many urban schools, school prayer, school desegregation, job discrimination and education, or aid to public/private higher education. Use readings and discussions on one of these topics to open up questions about how the realities of schooling and our judgments about learning institutions are connected to other cultural values and societal realities and how they have changed over time.

5. If a group of students is from a similar ethnic, racial, or religious background or is of the same gender—or if a number of different groups are represented in the class—ask students to research the educational history of their group and its social and economic implications.

6. Have students write about their ideal school/learning situation. Focus on the values, assumptions, and nature of these ideals; then compare these models with other utopian educational designs and experiments throughout history. Joel Spring, *A Primer of Libertarian Education*, provides a good overview of the ideals of such utopian projects, as does chapter 7 of Theodore Roszak, *Person/Planet*, and the case study in Eliot Wigginton's *Sometimes a Shining Moment: The Foxfire Experience*.

7. Have students examine curricula and definitions of an "educated person" throughout history. (The wider the historical period, the better.) Discuss the kinds of changes they see, the reasons for these changes, and the ways definitions and purposes of education have changed over time.

8. Ask students to research the university system in another culture and/or to research the ways in which learning is defined or categorized in a society very different from their own. Use this as a basis for writing and discussion on the ways in which students' learning would be thought about, valued, and interpreted differently in different social contexts. Thomas R. Rohlen, *Japan's High Schools*, is a good source, as is Nigel Grant, *Soviet Education*. One resource that contains materials on a number of school systems is Edward Ignas and Raymond Corsini, *Comparative Educational Systems*.

9. Ask students to read a number of the recent commission reports of the state of American education today, such as *Action for Excellence* by the Education Commission of the States, *A Nation at Risk* by the National Commission on Excellence in Education, or *America's Competitive Challenge* by the Business Higher Education Forum. Offering somewhat different perspectives are John Goodlad, *A Place Called School*, Theodore Sizer, *Horace's Compromise*; and Gerald Grant, *The World We Created at Hamilton High*. Focus on the similarities and differences in their findings and recommendations and on the significance of these reports to the ways in which we think about the role of schools in our society. Two helpful secondary sources are Beatrice and Ronald Gross, eds., *The Great School Debate: Which Way for American Education?* and Philip Altbach et al., eds., *Excellence in Education*.

E. Case Study: Samuel Morris

Samuel Morris, the son of poor rural farmers in the Mississippi delta, is a railway employee who rose from the ranks to become a supervisor. After thirty-five years he is retiring with a good pension. The pride of his life is having raised his children to be professionals; through his own and his wife's hard work he has enabled them to receive the education he was denied. His son is a college professor and his daughter a physician. "Now," Samuel says, "it's Papa's turn."

Samuel is entering college with a complex set of feelings about education. On the one hand he has a healthy sense of anger at the traditional denial of educational opportunity in his community and how that denial has been used to limit social and employment options. Much of his pride in his and his children's achievements arises from this historical perspective. He has, however, internalized a sense of his own ignorance and feels a bit left behind by his children's success.

Exploring the meaning of education can help Samuel in several ways. First, it can affirm his understanding of the role of education in his own community and of the use and misuse of education within broad social, economic, and political contexts. Whatever his ethnic origins, it may be interesting for him to read fiction and nonfiction works on the role of education in his community. If he is still laboring under a sense of failure concerning his early schooling, he may be interested in Jonathan Kozol, *Why Children Fail*, or a similar work.

Further, by broadening his definition of education, this approach may help Samuel understand how much he has learned in his life in spite of a lack of formal schooling. At the same time it will expose him to the wealth of knowledge now available to him. Once he can see that his unfamiliarity with aspects of human culture is not a mark of his own failure, he can choose freely among areas of study.

In many ways Samuel is in an enviable position. As a student, he is free of financial and career pressures and can, if he likes, spend his time studying whatever interests him. At the same time, his enthusiasm for education may well save him from the boredom and isolation that afflicts so many retirees. This approach offers him a good start because it allows him greater perspective on his own experience while fostering a new sense of his right to study whatever he chooses.

A. Introduction

B ecause many adults enter college at critical transition points in their lives, their work experiences serve not only as the foundation of their prior learning but as their major reason for returning to school. Going to college means the opportunity to think about their interests, about job transition, about careers. For these students, schooling and careers are intimately intertwined. Access to reliable information and guidance in decisionmaking about careers are important aspects of such students' education.

Students who come to college in this situation can find in the portfolio development course an opportunity to examine their present employment systematically and to assess future career opportunities clearly and realistically. In this approach students can develop a fuller understanding of competencies they already possess, think about new areas of learning necessary for various career choices, and get information about the job market and projected employment trends. For students who have not been employed outside of the home, who have been out of the workforce for a number of years, or who are facing lay-off, this approach offers a mutually supportive environment in which to explore work options and articulate needs.

Compiling a portfolio using this approach serves both as an opportunity to think about the connections between education and work and as an exercise in compiling a resume. Its more pragmatic focus is also important for students who have come to college with very specific work-related needs and who can use the course to deepen their understanding of educational and employment options and opportunities.

B. When to Use this Approach

The major advantage to this approach is that students can discover and explore ways in which identifying their interests and skills can help them to think about career options. So, too, the development of the portfolio can be interconnected with the creation of a detailed skills resume often needed for employment searches. The recognition of prior learning and present expertise can also help to sustain and encourage students in difficult or transitional employment situations. Finally, as with the two approaches that follow, the "Careers" approach provides an organic way to explore the relationship between academic knowledge and workplace activity.

This approach works best when

- the instructor is an experienced career counselor who is aware of realistic employment trends and the need to distinguish between encouragement and false expectations;

- assignments help students not to personalize structural economic transitions but to understand their particular situations within broader social, economic, and cultural terms; and

- within the vocational focus, instructors are able to help students evaluate the need for broadly based competencies and focused technical training.

C. Sample Topics to be Covered

1. Experiential learning and job-transferable skills.

2. Education and work.

3. The current job market and projected employment trends.

4. Exploration of personal interests, requirements, and goals.

5. Skill, competency, and degree requirements for identified employment possibilities.

D. Sample Assignments and Activities

1. Assign and guide students through the process of self-assessment and educational and career planning using one of the recognized books in the field. Possible titles include Richard Bolles, *What Color Is Your Parachute?*; George Ford and Gordon Lippitt, *Planning Your Future: A Workbook for Personal Goal Setting*; Bernard Haldane, *Career Satisfaction and Success*; John Holland, *The Self-Directed Search: A Guide to Educational and Vocational Planning*; and Barbara Sher, *Wishcraft*.

2. Help students to work through one of the many good self-assessment tools for identifying interests, values, and skills. These include the following.

- The Strong-Campbell Interest Inventory and the Self-Directed Search, both developed by John Holland. The Self-Directed Search is popular because it is self-scoring and because the results can then be matched to a small reference book of occupational titles. The Strong-Campbell is usually sent away to be scored and matched to career possibilities, although a newer version can be computer-scored immediately.

- SIGI-PLUS, developed and owned by the Educational Testing Service, is leased by many college and community counseling services. SIGI-PLUS is one of a number of interactive computer systems in which answers to questions direct the program to move in a variety of responsive directions. It allows the user to identify critical values, important skills, and interests in order to develop rational process for making career choices.

- DISCOVER FOR ADULTS is owned by American College Testing Services and leased by many schools and counseling centers and, occasionally, major corporate employers. This system also allows users to identify values, skills, and interests, with the emphasis on skills. The profile is matched to a "World of Work" map listing hundreds of careers.

3. Assign readings and/or schedule speakers on the current job market and projected employment trends and have students regularly consult documents such as the *Monthly Labor Review*. Challenge students to find materials that offer contrasting perspectives and projections.

4. Ask students to describe the "perfect" job. Work with them to identify those qualities or components that make the job attractive to them and to research the range of jobs and careers that possess those qualities and components.

5. Once students have identified several possible careers, ask them to interview people currently engaged in them. Interview questions should center on the day-to-day reality of the job as opposed to the outsider's view and on the typical tasks, satisfactions, and frustrations of the job. The very process of developing a questionnaire, however informal, can help students to identify their own concerns and value judgments.

6. Where possible, ask unemployed students or students not yet returned to the job market to spend several days with people currently doing the jobs in which they are interested.

7. Through class discussion, identify the range of skills required in many types of employment— human relations skills, communication skills, etc. Work with students to identify the job-transferable skills they have developed through their previous paid and unpaid work.

8. Using a two-pronged approach to the portfolio development process, help students write a detailed skills resume that parallels the portfolio they are compiling. Discuss how previous skills development and training provide the basis both for college-accreditable learning and job-transferable skills.

E. Case Study: Patricia Tamase

Patricia Tamase grew up in a community in which women were given few career role models and in which their love of children was the operant value. She is now a teacher's aide who is being threatened with lay-off unless she earns an associate's degree. She has recently entered college and is determined to go on further for a bachelor's and a master's degree. She talks of becoming a teacher, a child psychologist, or a child welfare worker once she has completed her studies.

Patricia needs three things which the "Careers" approach can give her. The first is broad knowledge of child-related careers. Patricia knows of only those career options she has herself observed in the schools and her community; she might never think, for example, of being an attorney specializing in children's rights. Second, she needs exposure to other fields and a sense of herself beyond the single value of loving and caring for children. Finally, she needs an opportunity to discover the skills, talents, and strengths she has and that she will bring with her into any field.

Patricia's writing of her portfolio, in this case, can be part of a more general exploration of her values and aptitudes. Any of a number of books such as *What Color Is Your Parachute* or *The Self-Directed Search* can help focus this process, as can a variety of computer-based systems such as SIGI-PLUS. Parallel to the uncovering of talents and interests can be an exposure to career possibilities both within and outside of child-related fields. Since Patricia's most comfortable way of learning at this point is probably through face-to-face contact, much of her career exploration can be structured around interviews with professionals and visits to job sites.

Unlike Joanna Smith, but like most wage-earning women, Patricia has no choice as to whether or not she works; her family needs her income. Her examination of career possibilities and her own talents, therefore, must walk a fine line. On the one hand Patricia's sense of her possibilities does not need to be limited— it already is. On the other hand, however, her decision making must be informed by concrete and accurate information about the job market and the educational expectations of various fields.

Interestingly, the portfolio Patricia produces during the workshop may ultimately be of less practical value to her than other products that can come out of the same exercises. Given her current level of academically quantifiable skills, the assessment process itself may provide her with relatively few college credits. What the same process will enable her to do, however, is to compile detailed skill and experience resumes for use in identifying strengths and opportunities. These can also form the basis of job-search resumes when the time comes.

INTRODUCTION TO A FIELD

A. Introduction

Many adults return to school for upgrading and receiving credentials in fields in which they have worked for many years. Their knowledge of their fields and the close relationship between their prior learning and chosen course of college study make them prime candidates for an approach that links portfolio development with curriculum planning. Examples of such students are licensed practical nurses entering a B.S. program in nursing, auto workers in a robotics or auto mechanics program, and union leaders earning a labor studies degree.

For students who already have a good deal of college-level learning in their chosen fields, the portfolio development workshop can be combined with an "Introduction to . . ." course in the field itself. This approach allows students to pursue an in-depth exploration of their specific educational needs, but in the context of an overview of the current state of organization, knowledge, and technology in their field. They can view the structure of the field as a whole, become aware of the relationship between work and knowledge, and understand the role of new knowledge and technological change in the future.

This approach is, in effect, a more focused version of the "Careers" approach. Because these students have already chosen a course of study, however, their explorations can be more specific to one academic, professional, or technical field. The greater specificity allows for a deeper and more systematic exploration.

Compiling a portfolio using this approach allows students to reflect on their knowledge in a conceptual and professional context and gain perspective both on what they already know and on what they need to learn while in school. They can come to see their prior learning as part of the collective lore of a working community and view their planned course of study in the context of the evolution of the field as a whole.

B. When to Use This Approach

The basic advantage of this approach is that the relationship between prior and future learning is organically established. Adult students are recognized as already expert and active participants in their fields; thus the relationship between instructor and students is that of fellow members of a community of knowledge. A further advantage is that this approach can also encourage extremely job focused students to view their work in broader academic, professional, and societal terms.

This approach works best when

- students are from the same or closely related fields and working toward similar goals;
- the course is taught by a faculty member in the students' field; and
- professional and technical knowledge is both understood as significant in its own right and linked to more conventional liberal studies.

C. Sample Topics to Be Covered

1. The meaning of experiential learning.
2. Work and knowledge in the students' field.
3. The role of theoretical and practical knowledge.
4. The field as academic discipline and practical activity.
5. The history, current realities, and anticipated trends of the field.
6. The history and future of technology and skill in the field.
7. Ethical dilemmas in the field confronting practitioners and society.
8. Design of a course of study within the field.

D. Sample Assignments and Activities

1. Ask students to compile an annotated resume of jobs and assignments they have had in their field or industry, detailing the job functions they have fulfilled and the activities they have carried out.

2. In a writing assignment or small group activity, ask students to imagine they have been going to school rather than working all these years and that their activities have been for the purpose of learning, not earning a living. Ask them to identify the "curriculum" of their "schools." Have them compile an autobiography or annotated

resume in which they use the words "I learned" and "they taught me" rather than "I did" and "I was assigned."

3. Ask students to develop a detailed description of the workforce at their place of employment based on the *knowledge* different jobs require and the *authority* that comes with each job. Then help them to make connections between these different kinds of knowledge and skill and the different kinds of jobs that people hold.

4. Using various sources, such as assigned readings and descriptions of course offerings, ask students to identify the courses, departments, and academic disciplines relevant to their current jobs and to other jobs in the field.

5. Ask students to interview someone who holds the job for which they are educating themselves. Interview questions might include

- the person's experience of and reflections on his or her schooling;
- the day-to-day reality of the job—tasks, satisfactions, frustrations;
- the relationship between the training and the day-to-day job, including the use of theoretical versus practical education; and
- the person's felt need for further training.

6. Invite guest lecturers who are theoreticians and practitioners in the field.

7. Assign readings on

- the analysis and overview of the field;
- theory of prior learning and the workplace as a source of knowledge;
- the need for theoretical and practical learning;
- the history of the field or industry; and
- the history of skill, credentialing, and educational requirements in the field.

Whatever the readings, the goal here is to help students draw links between their practical learning and the broader theoretical, historical, socioeconomic, and cultural dimensions of their past and future studies.

8. Ask students to read selections from an introductory text in their field. Use this as an opportunity for students to reflect upon their own knowledge and to distinguish between the process and content of experientially gained knowledge versus that of formal academic learning.

E. Case Study: John Martin

John Martin worked his way up from the ranks in a construction firm, serving as subforeman, foreman, and now general manager. In the process, he has taught himself accounting, bookkeeping, production management, and construction materials utilization. Because of changing technology and business patterns, many small firms like John's are going out of business. Fearing that the business will close, John wants to strengthen his employability by getting a degree. He has entered a college that awards credits for experiential learning and has begun the course focused on getting every credit he can, wishing to get a degree in construction management as quickly as possible.

Clearly, John has very focused ambitions—too focused, perhaps. He knows the field is changing, and he is committed to preparing for the future. He has not taken the time to research these changes, however, and so does not have enough information with which to make informed educational choices.

"The Introduction to a Field" approach can help John do this important preliminary work. While no one can provide him with a perfect blueprint for future success, a great deal of information is available on the social and economic trends that affect the construction industry. Readings on changing business patterns and organizational structures can inform John of the kinds of management positions that are likely to become available and the educational backgrounds needed for them. Readings on the new technology in the industry will provide further data on educational requirements and desirable skills.

The research John does into the future trends in his field can have the second benefit of showing him how much he knows already. On one level, of course, he knows this; he knows he can translate his years of experience into college credit. But he is likely to be less sure of his expertise when looking toward the future and at the "young kids" right out of computer schools and MBA programs. Writing his portfolio in the context of industry needs will allow him to recognize his advantages.

It will at the same time help him identify what he needs to learn. Initially, John may define his educational needs somewhat narrowly; he may even insist that he needs no further knowledge at all, but only the "piece of paper." John may not be aware of aspects of his job that one can study at college; he may have only a limited understanding of fields such as industrial psychology, personnel management, or construction safety and health. And he may have little appreciation of the role of liberal arts and theoretical studies in preparing for future employment. This approach is different from the "College Orientation" approach used with Mary Roberts in that here the aim is to develop scope and perspective within a particular field rather than to use previous experience merely as a starting point.

An "introduction" to the construction field seems an ironic choice of approach for someone with John's experience. But introducing it as a field of academic study within the context of a changing reality will help improve John's employability—his motive for going to school.

THE EXPERIENCE OF WORK

A. Introduction

For many of our students, work in a particular field has been at the heart of their learning. Sometimes they have accumulated impressive amounts and great depth of knowledge in their area of expertise. But often, even in its strength, this kind of learning may lack context—a social, historical, and political grounding that allows students to think about their experience and learning in a more all-encompassing way.

These students can find in the portfolio development course an opportunity to explore the wider circumstances, issues, and problems that have informed their work lives. In this approach, students can become more familiar with the history of the industries to which they belong or the changes in work life over time. More broadly, the nature and quality of work itself and the role of work in human life can serve as a central theme, encouraging students to examine their experiences in a new light.

Although the workplace is again a major focus, this approach is quite different from ''Careers'' or ''Introduction to a Field.'' Rather than helping to structure a career-oriented education, it serves as an introduction to social and humanistic studies by encouraging students to view their own lives from a variety of perspectives. A parallel approach focusing on the family or the community offers a similar overview for students whose work lives have been spent primarily in the home or in volunteer community work.

Compiling a portfolio using this approach allows students to place themselves within a broader social-historical constellation and to become more cognizant of the factors that have affected people's work lives. Such an approach may be particularly significant for those students with much technical/professional expertise but relatively little experience dealing with the questions and approaches of liberal studies.

B. When to Use This Approach

This approach allows technical and more career-oriented students to broaden their perspectives on work and the role of work in human life through sociological, historical, and cross-cultural study. It also gives students the opportunity to articulate pride in their skills and in their jobs whether or not their prior learning is accreditable in a particular institution. Here, liberal and theoretical studies can be introduced and worked with as approaches that arise from students' own lives rather than as alien and artificial fields of inquiry.

This approach works best when

- work is a central component of the lives and expectations of students' past experiences and future expectations;

- instructors give attention and respect to all types of paid and unpaid labor, including the volunteer work many women have performed and the contributions retired people continue to make;

- instructors remain cognizant of their own value judgments of different types of work as well as the value judgments of their students; and

- distinctions are carefully explored between valuable and admirable workplace skills and those that are considered accreditable as college-level learning.

C. Sample Topics to Be Covered

1. The history of work and of attitudes toward work.

2. The experience of work.

3. Race, class, and gender in the workforce.

4. The sociology of status, recognition, alienation, and pride.

5. The history of technology.

6. The relationship of work to society, domestic policy, and international relations.

7. Portrayals of work and workers in philosophy, literature, and fine arts.

D. Sample Assignments and Activities

1. Ask students to write a history of their occupations during their own working lifetimes, mentioning only those changes and events

they have participated in or been affected by directly. Have them use themselves as examples of how the occupation, its workers, its technology, its products and services, and its customers have changed. Subsequent group discussions of such transformations can provide an even broader portrait of change across industries or in the economy as a whole.

2. Ask students to interview retired workers in their fields and to compile a history based on their own experiences, the retirees' experiences, and the differences between the two. For older workers, it may be more interesting to interview newcomers.

3. Assign readings on the history, sociology, and economics of the workplace and of students' individual jobs. These might include studies that emphasize comparisons across industries, historical periods, and nations.

4. Discuss readings from fiction and poetry on work, workers, and the students' individual jobs. "The Office I Work In," a chapter from Joseph Heller, *Something Happened*, is a good starting point, as is Rebecca Harding Davis' nineteenth-century novel, *Life in the Iron Mills*. Similarly, the class can view representations from the plastic and performing arts that portray attitudes toward and experiences of work.

5. Ask students to write descriptions of their jobs and workplace experiences. Use the descriptions to arrive at definitions of work satisfaction, human needs for recognition and self-expression, quality of work life, and related issues. Theoretical works on the meaning of alienation and job satisfaction can be brought in here as well: *Work in America: Report of a Special Task Force to the Secretary of Health, Education, and Welfare* is one possible text, as are David Jenkins, *Job Power*; Erich Fromm, *The Sane Society*; and part 3 of Bertell Ollman, *Alienation*. Also relevant are texts concerning "women's work," such as Ann Oakley, *Women's Work: The Housewife, Past, Present, and Future* and Louise Howe, *Pink Collar Workers: Inside the World of Women's Work*.

6. Ask students to address the issue of technology in one of a variety of ways. They may research current and future technological change in their industry; respond to such cinematic interpretations of technology as Chaplin's *Modern Times*, *Star Wars*, and *2001*; or analyze how a specific technological development has affected American economic and foreign policy.

Important texts on the changing role of technology are Robert Howard, *Brave New Workplace*; Richard Edwards, *Contested Terrain: The Transformation of the Workplace in the Twentieth Century*; Donald Kennedy, Charles Craypo, and Mary Lehman, *Labor and Technology*; Shoshana Zuboff, *In the Age of the Smart Machine*; and Harley Shaiken, *Work Transformed: Automation and Labor in the Computer Age*.

E. Case Study: Frank Hersh

Frank Hersh is a telephone worker studying substance abuse counseling. As a lineman for the local telephone company, he knows that he may soon be facing a job loss and is interested in turning his many years as a leader in his union's substance abuse program into an alternate career. He is willing to take the pay cut that might be initially require, but he does need to train himself, as he says, "for a sure thing."

Frank, to be sure, is frightened for himself and for his own job prospects should lay-offs occur. But he is equally frightened by the heightened stress of job insecurity and economic change is doing to his fellow workers. He can measure the change clearly in the rise of substance abuse within the workforce, and he knows that other stress-related symptoms must also be increasing. Frank is thus returning to school with a double mission—to improve his own chances for continued employment while doing something to help others who need it.

"The Experience of Work" approach presents an interesting perspective on both aspects of Frank's studies. The portfolio itself will keep separate Frank's two kinds of skill: telephone technology and substance abuse counseling. But the course can allow him to view the two as parts of a whole. Both to come to terms with his own job insecurity and to understand the stress of his fellow workers, Frank needs a social and economic perspective on what has happened in his industry and why the lay-offs are occurring. Perhaps even more important, he needs a concrete understanding of the place of work in people's lives and the threat to their sense of self posed by job insecurity, deskilling, and unemployment. Readings in these areas as well as discussions with his fellow students will be helpful to him.

Frank is in a difficult position as a worker, but as a student his situation is oddly fortuitous. For most students, the transition to academic modes of thought and inquiry necessitates a new understanding of the relationship between theory and practice and between social reality and individual experience. Frank needs that understanding as well, but the changes in Frank's industry make that lesson both immediate and to the point. Frank and his coworkers are themselves central cases in point of the effect on the individual of changes in the larger society.

A. Introduction

Depending on the structures and academic policies of their institutions, students have varying input into the actual design of their individual curricula. For students in some colleges, assessment exists within the parameters of predefined curricula. Other students, however, have the freedom to choose among a wide variety of courses, methods of study, and schools.

Students who can participate in the design of their own college curriculum find in the portfolio development course an opportunity to examine the broad learning options they have. In this approach, they can research academic programs, speak with professionals in various fields, and pursue any activities that can help them define their academic goals and translate them into a viable program design. Students can be challenged not only to describe specific topics of future study but to be attentive to the interconnections among these topics and to search for common themes and questions that may serve as a thread within their program.

Compiling a portfolio using this approach can help students to articulate their own individual goals with care and to communicate them to others. It can also offer students a fine opportunity to work across disciplinary boundaries and to think thematically. In addition, students will be challenged to examine curriculum development itself and to learn about the kinds of criteria that can be applied to the evaluation of an academically "sound" set of studies.

B. When to Use this Approach

"The Degree Design" approach allows much individual student input and encourages independence of research and thought. It also has the advantage of serving as a clear link between the evaluation of prior learning and the development of a program or curriculum. Students also have the opportunity to think about an array of academic issues that may help them hone their goals. Finally, students complete the course with a very personal sense of accomplishment and of ownership of and control over their educational plans.

This approach works best when

- assignments emphasize research and exploration of individual student interests or else where assessment is conducted as a series of individual counseling sessions;

- students are well-motivated, have a high level of interest, and are somewhat experienced in active decision-making; and

- instructors are willing to work patiently with much diversity and to be able to coordinate a variety of particular orientations and projects.

C. Sample Topics to be Covered

1. General academic expectations in a world of specialization.

2. Philosophies of curriculum design.

3. The history of and critical issues in specific disciplines.

4. Philosophies and methods of defining and solving problems.

5. Thematic and interdisciplinary approaches to individualized degree design.

D. Sample Assignments and Activities

1. Ask students to find two or three current articles or essays that touch on points of interest to them. Assign them the task of drawing up a list of questions, problems, and topics of study that flow from these readings. Use these issues as the basis for clarifying areas of interest and identifying additional subjects that they might want to study in greater depth.

2. Ask students to define an "educated person" and to identify what areas they would need to study to "become" such a person. Help them to connect these topics to each other and to possible courses of study available.

3. Using college catalogs, have students analyze the degree requirements of a variety of institutions. Discuss the educational values implicit in each set of requirements and the ways in which they define an "educated person."

4. Have students write about their past learning and interests in a descriptive way. After a discussion (and/or readings) of the scope of various fields of inquiry, such as history, psychology, sociology, literature, philosophy, and science, ask them to create a map in which they draw some initial connections between their learning and interests and these other fields/orientations.

5. Focus a number of exercises on the whole issue of how colleges have developed curricula. This can entail studying a general text on curriculum development, reading a number of the recent national reports on basic educational requirements, or closely examining many different curricula from different university settings and departments. The aim here is to help students think about how people drew up these programs, what assumptions they made, and what goals and ideals they may have had in mind. Ask students to consider their own curricular assumptions about what should be included and excluded.

6. As part of the preceding activity, have students read contrasting interpretations of curricular requirements. William Bennett's NEH report, "To Reclaim the Legacy," in the 28 November, 1984 edition of *The Chronicle of Higher Education* might be read along with Elizabeth Fox-Genovese, "The Great Tradition and Its Orphans, or Why the Defense of the Traditional Curriculum Requires the Restoration of Those It Excluded," in *The Rights of Memory*. Similarly, Adrienne Rich, "Towards a Woman-Centered University," *Women and the Power to Change* might be compared with Mortimer J. Adler, *The Paideia Proposal*. Research on the debate over the Stanford University core curriculum would be another useful introduction to these issues.

7. Create a number of hypothetical student "portraits," accentuating various personal histories and educational interests and goals. Use these as bases for discussion in which the group "helps" these "students" develop academic programs that meet their needs.

E. Case Study: Phyllis Mahoney

Phyllis Mahoney is an administrative assistant with the parks department of a major city. She has studied typing and stenography at a business academy; learned office management, bookkeeping, and purchasing on the job; and obtained a great deal of knowledge about urban administration and the structure of local government. She now realizes that she has come as far as she can in her job without a degree.

In recent years, Phyllis has attended a traditional community college. She has completed her work in writing, math, and research skills and has taken general courses in sociology and American history. In addition, she has been majoring in recreation management, the closest major she could find to the work she wants to do in the parks department.

Phyllis has realized, however, that the courses in recreation management are too technical and administratively oriented to satisfy her; she wants the degree and the job advancement, to be sure, but her intellectual interests are broader. "Parks are so important to people," she says. "Immigrants came to this country dreaming of all those great open spaces. Now for most of us, the parks are all that's left." She has decided to enter a nontraditional college that offers a wide range of educational services for adults, including individualized degree design and independent study.

For a student like Phyllis, the "Degree Design" approach is perfect. It can give her an opportunity to discover not only what she already knows about those "great open spaces" but what there still is to learn. Based on her discovery of educational possibilities and her exploration of her own interests, she can design a course of study that builds on her prior learning and focuses on her needs. No single academic discipline will be able to give Phyllis access to all the information she seeks, but she has rich possibilities for interdisciplinary study and for a quite personal integration of many avenues of inquiry. She may, for example, plan to further her general knowledge of urban government and her community college work in recreational management by studying recreational architecture and planning, spatial design and parks services, and the like. At the same time, she may plan to build on her previous work in sociology and history and her interests in the human aspects of park usage in such studies as urban sociology, the sociology of leisure, the role of community in American life, the ideal of nature in American culture, and urban culture and demographics.

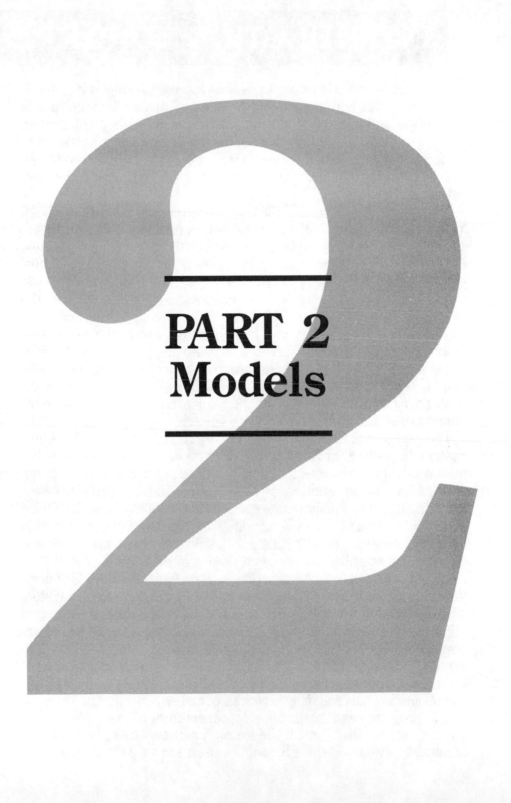

PART 2
Models

INTRODUCTION TO PART 2

The first section of this book presents approaches to portfolio development that both respond to the personal and professional needs of students and encourage substantive academic inquiry. Inherent in the varied goals of portfolio development is a significant opportunity for faculty and students not only to reflect on past learning but to use that reflection as a touchstone for educational planning and future college studies.

What has been presented thus far, however, has necessarily been hypothetical in nature. While it has been our intention to introduce a wide range of concrete approaches to portfolio development courses, these approaches truly come to life only within the context of actual practice. Part 2 of this book focuses on such working models.

For almost twenty years, institutions of higher education across the United States have been designing and implementing portfolio development courses. The faculty and administrators involved have experimented with alternative structures, created and revised syllabi, and, in the process, evolved a whole new area of academic practice. This ongoing experimentation over time has itself been a source of experiential learning, in which theory has often followed practice and in which our students have often been our teachers.

The institutions that have been involved run the gamut of American higher education: from small, private institutions to large state systems; from residential campuses to external degree programs; from community colleges to universities. In some cases, these institutions have their origins in the educational experimentation of the early 1970s and an explicit commitment to nontraditional students. Others have only recently focused on new populations of students for whom the evaluation of prior learning is central to academic endevor.

Part 2 of this volume consists of essays on fourteen models of portfolio development courses, written by the faculty and administrators who designed and teach them. Taken as a group, they point to real efforts to respond to the learning needs of adults, many of whom are new to the culture of higher education. Yet what is perhaps most exciting about the descriptions that follow is their serious attention to an abiding set of questions about the very nature of academic learning and about the goals and daily practices of higher education in America.

The programs and institutions represented here were chosen for a variety of reasons. First, while we have neither focused on nor systematically evaluated the procedures used for assessment, each of the programs follows the principles of good practice formulated by the Council for Adult and Experiential Learning in order to maintain rigorous academic standards in the evaluation of prior learning.[1]

Second, we have attempted to represent the eight approaches to portfolio development within a wide variety of academic contexts. Each of the approaches described in Part 1 forms the core of at least one of the course designs that follow. In addition, some of our contributors have adapted their models to particular populations of adult students: human service workers, women, urban or trade union activists, residents of the inner city. Others have molded their courses to fit specific institutional settings: external degree and distance learning modes, for example, or assessment programs shared institutions.

None of the courses described in this section conforms exactly to the approaches presented in Part 1. Rather, the institutions represented here have already done what we encourage all institutions to do, namely, to meld the possibilities into a unique course design suited to a particular institutional situation. We hope their example captures the seriousness and excitement of the endeavor to use portfolio development courses to enrich the theory and practice that inform our work as educators.

---

[1]*For a thorough discussion of the principles of good practice in the assessment of prior learning, see Urban Whittaker,* Assessing Learning: Standards, Principles and Procedures *(Philadelphia: CAEL, 1989).*

In this first essay, Brenda Krueger describes the portfolio development course conducted by the Credit for Lifelong Learning Program of Sinclair Community College in Dayton, Ohio. A combination of the "Personal Exploration" and "Careers" approaches, CLLP allows students' life goals and career decisions to provide the organizing framework for credit requests. "Structuring requests for prior learning assessment around a student's goals," Krueger argues, "ensures that the accredited experiential learning . . . bears direct relevance . . . to the student's degree."

SINCLAIR COMMUNITY COLLEGE

Brenda Krueger

In 1976, Sinclair Community College founded a new program, the Credit for Lifelong Learning Program to meet the needs of a new, nontraditional student body then coming through its doors. Then, as now, over half of the 17,000 students attending SCC each year were more than twenty-five years old. These students came from many class backgrounds and represented all of the intellectual, social, and ethnic communities of Dayton, Ohio. Their psychographics—their accomplishments, needs, wants, ambitions, and goals—were equally diverse.

Serving these individuals in the traditional way developed for a homogeneous group of eighteen-year-old students was clearly inappropriate. First, the motives of these adult students and their feelings upon embarking on higher education differed from those of traditional students. Second, many shared a sense of urgency and felt frustrated when they looked ahead at years of part-time college. As one adult student said at the time: "I've got to get rolling . . . I'm running behind! Don't waste my time with stuff I already know."

To help such older students "get rolling" and avoid "wasting their time with stuff they already know," the faculty and administrators at Sinclair Community College designed and implemented the Credit for Lifelong Learning Program to enable adult students to earn credits for prior, off-campus experiential learning. CLLP used a portfolio assessment process as the primary mode of prior learning assessment and the faculty of the Experience Based Education Department as the primary support network for students engaged in the process. The methods currently used by CLLP faculty and their evolution provide an interesting case study in the nature of lifelong learning and of the adult students who continue to take advantage of programs like CLLP.

The original design for the portfolio development phase of CLLP was based on two prevailing assumptions gleaned from the literature on adult learners. The first assumption was that adults are experiential learners who typically prefer active rather than passive modes of learning. The second was that these same adults are also self-directed learners who fare best when allowed to plan and direct their own learning on an individual basis. Participants in CLLP were therefore given the opportunity to work with a portfolio development faculty member on a one-to-one basis, and they had the freedom to work autonomously on their portfolios and to pace themselves as they wished.

However clear-cut the theory, it soon became apparent that the program was inadequate to the needs of the students it was designed to serve. Although as many as one thousand adults entered the program per year, only about 50 percent completed a portfolio satisfactorily during the first four years of the program's existence. This led the CLLP faculty to reexamine the validity of the assumptions upon which CLLP had been based.

In effect, our experience indicated that only one of our two assumptions about adult learners was correct. As expected, many of these students had chosen in the past to learn experientially—through work, volunteer activities, and hobbies—and had avoided college. As one student wrote, experience, not higher education, appealed to her. She explained, "I wanted to travel, go places, see things." Another typical student explained that he "had little desire to attend college." Instead, he wanted "a career" and had decided to attend college only because he "realized the importance of higher education as it relates to industry and my profession." Repeatedly, adults' portfolios reflected this preference for learning experientially.

Thus, our first assumption, that of the experiential nature of much adult learning, was borne out by the responses of our students. The second, however, that of self-directed adult learning, was not. The learning experiences that students brought to the program typically involved direction by someone else, perhaps a supervisor or workshop leader. A review of former students' portfolios illustrated this fact. When the majority of these students described their learning experiences, they used such phrases as "I was required to learn the physical features of the 425 computer . . ." or "My supervisor sent me to a class. This class was three weeks long, with attendance required eight hours per day . . ." Many CLLP students were accustomed to a certain amount of external direction and structure and, it seemed likely, would welcome that direction and structure here, especially since the CLL program was in many cases their first college experience.

An honest look at CLLP revealed that the structure and support that students seemed to need was missing from the portfolio development process. Although students began the process with a credit-bearing course called Portfolio Development, this course involved only two or three group sessions and relied heavily on extensive individual advising and self-paced efforts by students. Ironically, the opportunity for focus, flexibility, and independence it offered worked against the very students it was designed to benefit. The lack of firm deadlines, for example, established out of respect for the busy lives of adults, made it more difficult for students to structure their time. Similarly, the total focus on the individual sacrificed opportunities for adult students to interact with their peers and form a support system. Moreover, with each student's isolation, there was no opportunity for active discovery in the process, in spite of our explicitly stated belief that adults frequently prefer to learn experientially, to make discoveries.

Further, our examination revealed that the structure and mode of delivery were not the only weaknesses in the program. The CLLP faculty also identified particular pitfalls that often contributed to student attrition. Specifically, there was no strategy for addressing adults' typical lack of confidence in their experiential learning or in their own ability to set and meet goals. The staff felt that very few students had dropped out of the process because they lacked sufficient college-level learning; rather, they believed that because the design had not fostered commitment to and comfort with the process, many gave up as soon as they encountered a problem.

Confronting these issues, the CLLP faculty redesigned the portfolio development process to make it more structured and more experiential and to overcome the predictable pitfalls confronting students. Three-hour classroom sessions each week became the main mode of instruction, and a detailed course syllabus was written that clearly stated the weekly objectives and student assignments. There was also an extremely explicit and detailed student guide that, if necessary, could supply all the information a student would need to create a portfolio. In this way, structure was built into the process. To supply the other key component that had been missing—the experiential component—the CLLP faculty added in-class activities.

The intent of the current version of the portfolio development course is to move students step by step toward the goal of completing a portfolio of their prior learning. Specifically, the objective is a portfolio that includes 1) a section stating the student's goals, 2) a chronological record of important events in the student's life, 3) a narrative life history discussing the impact of the most significant events, 4) a description of past experiences and the learning from them as it relates to specific course competency areas, and 5) documentation to verify the quality of the experiences and the learning.

Students in CLLP, however, do not only articulate prior learning; they are expected to acquire *new*, college level learning as a result of the course. They learn how to develop life and career goals and an action plan for making those goals a reality. It is equally important that they develop the ability to extract learning from experiences, a skill that has applications in their future as well as their past. The articulation of old learning and the acquisition of new learning are not viewed as two separate educational goals; the ability to analyze meaning, to perceive relevance and purpose, and to articulate process, cause and effect, and other patterns are all intellectual attainments that come directly out of the work of portfolio development.

The role of the faculty in this process of self-discovery and self-articulation is to keep students committed to the process and to help them overcome the pitfalls that interfered with completion in the past. Activities and assignments that lead to accomplishing these goals are woven together so that, frequently, an activity or assignment contributes to the achievement of several objectives at once.

To illustrate, the central objectives of the first week of the course are for students to understand CLLP's operation and to be able to create their chronological records and life history papers. Yet the first week's in-class activities have other purposes, too.

For instance, the first activity used in the first class session is a sentence completion exercise. In it, two students form a dyad and alternately complete phrases such as, "The first impression I give to people is . . ."; "A talent or skill I haven't used in years is . . ."; "What makes me unique is . . ."; "If I really used the best skills that I have, the kind of work I would do is . . ." Completing some of the phrases encourages students to begin recognizing and verbalizing their abilities, helping to increase their confidence in their own experiential learning. At the same time, this interaction helps individuals in the class get to know one another and allows them to begin to form a support group, thus creating a sense of camaraderie among the class members that later serves to strengthen their commitment to completing their portfolios.

Another in-class activity that first week both further reinforces students' faith in their past learning and gives them a new opportunity to be active, experiential learners. Again, students form dyads. One member of the dyad is asked to pretend that he or she has just been promoted, the other hired to take over his or her previous duties. The defined task is to train the "replacement" to perform those duties. Then the roles are reversed. This training is of course impossible to accomplish in the brief time allotted. What does get accomplished, however, is that participants begin to discover how much they know.

Even the act of drafting the first week's outside assignments, the chronological record and the life history paper, yields new learning for students. Creating their chronological record triggers a myriad of memories about their experiences and requires that they begin to analyze those experiences, to identify their meaning, and to articulate their impact. Students learn that all experience is not equally significant, a first step in learning to extract learning from experience or to differentiate between them.

Before they can extract the learning from their experiences, however, students must decide what categories of learning they want to present for assessment. Because a single experience can yield many diverse kinds of learning, any student attempting to articulate experiential learning without such categories for guidance would face an overwhelming task. For example, a year of experience as a PTA president could provide learning about leadership, budgeting, marketing, conflict resolution, and child abuse, and other experiences offer similar variety. Since it is impossible to write about all the learning in an individual's life, a focus must be found.

It is the student's own life and career goals that determine that focus. For instance, the PTA president would focus on learning about conflict resolution and child abuse if he or she wished to pursue a degree in sociology, but would focus on learning related to leadership, budgeting, and marketing if the degree choice was management.

Introducing goal searching and life and career planning at this early stage yields important benefits. First, it provides a continuum between past learning and future studies. Structuring requests for prior learning assessment around a student's goals ensures that the accredited experiential learning is not random, but bears direct relevance to the student's studies at Sinclair Community College and to the student's degree.

Second, there is a practical benefit to grounding portfolio development in goal-searching activities; CLLP faculty have found that students who have clear goals are more likely to complete a portfolio successfully. Having a goal in sight seems to give students the impetus to move through the rigorous portfolio development process. Conversely, students who do not know their own reason for pursuing college credit, who do not articulate an educational aim, tend to give up when the real work of portfolio development begins.

For both of the reasons just stated, therefore, the in-class activities during the second and third weeks of the course are designed to help students learn how to discover, clarify, and articulate their life and career goals and to create a plan for achieving those goals. These goal-setting activities were developed specifically for this course and were structured to be as experiential as possible.

For years psychologists have understood that the imagination creates inner experiences that can be just as real as experiences in the external world. Moreover, the imaginary world has none of the limits of space and time that the "real" world has. In their experiential in-class activities, faculty and students are not restricted to the classroom or to the present, a real advantage in the goal-setting process.

The CLLP faculty shows students how to use their imaginations to simulate real-life experience as they begin to plan their futures. To do this, the faculty uses a technique called "guided imagery." The CLLP faculty member leads participants through a fantasy that can help them use their imaginations to discover new information about themselves, information they may have blocked from their conscious minds. Adults making life and career plans frequently have trouble recognizing the goals they really want to achieve because they cannot look beyond immediate barriers such as family responsibilities and current work obligations. Guided imagery is a method that enables students to ignore such barriers temporarily and imagine what their futures could be. Specifically, the CLLP faculty member leading a course takes students through an imagery developed for the course by educational consultant Anastas Harris, using the following words:

> Imagine a day in which you are all alone. You have the day to yourself to relax and enjoy, and you are relishing the thought of it. You go out to collect your mail and find that only one thing is delivered. It is an elegantly wrapped parcel addressed to you. You open the

parcel and find inside a beautiful leather-bound book. There is no card or return address identifying who sent the book to you. Your name is inscribed in gold on the front cover of the book. You gaze at the cover and experience the feelings it evokes. Slowly, you open the book and flip through the pages. You realize that this book is the story of your life. You stop at one page and begin to read about a day in your life when you felt really happy to be you. You are in touch with your strengths and beauty, your inner greatness. Remember that wonderful day. When you are finished, you flip over the pages again until you come to a page describing a day in your life ten years from now. What you read delights you, for you find that you have fully capitalized on your potential and either overcome or avoided your weaknesses. You are a self-realized being, living as you would most wish to live.

How are you living? What do you do? What kind of person have you become? What does the book say about the way you look and feel, about your family life, about your environment, your work life, your personal life, about your social life, and about the level of your affluence? You now begin to feel that you have read enough for the moment and close the book to savor what you have learned thus far.

Experience how you feel about what you have learned about your future. When you are ready, open your eyes, and return to the reality of today and this room.

After the imagery ends the faculty member asks students to refrain from talking and to write about their experiences immediately so they do not lose the images and the learning. Students are then given the chance to talk about the images. Finally, after the sharing, students and the faculty member discuss how the images—the dream—could become reality. They discuss how to set small objectives that when accomplished lead step by step to achieving the larger goals.

Overall, student feedback on the imagery experience has been encouraging. One student wrote, "I thought this class was one of the most enlightening classes I have ever had. I guess I forgot how to look into the future. Today taught me more than I have learned in a long time."[1]

---

[1]*Brenda Krueger, "Improving the Credit for Lifelong Learning Process with Halestic Education Techniques," in* New Directions for Experiential Learning—Building on Experiences in Adult Development, *ed. Betty Menson (San Francisco: Jossey-Bass, 1982), 93–96.*

Yet the guided imagery is not effective for every student. Some do not find techniques for tapping into their imaginations helpful. Still others get insight into their personal lives as a result of the exercise, but still need help clarifying their professional goals. Therefore, the CLLP faculty supplement the guided imagery with a totally different approach for looking into the students' future possibilities.

This approach, developed by Sinclair professor Mary Alice Geiselhart, requires students and the faculty member to play roles. The instructions are as follows:

> The instructor is to take the role of Vice-President of Human Resources for a large, affluent company which is going to provide some of its employees with an unusually desirable work situation. Students in the class are to think of themselves as employees of this corporation. The time is some time in the future when the students have graduated and are employed fulltime in the career they have chosen.
>
> They have been selected by the company to enjoy working conditions as close to ideal as the company can make them. The rationale for spending whatever is necessary to achieve ideal conditions is that under such conditions, the employee is most likely to produce maximally in a way that ultimately benefits the company, the employee, and even society.

With this in mind, students break into small groups of four to six people and given one condition: they can have these ideal working conditions only if everyone in the small group can agree on what such "ideal" conditions are. Students are then asked to define the ideal conditions on which they agree with regard to:

A. Working environment
  1. The Place
     a. geographic location
     b. kind of place (wilderness, midwestern suburb, near a city, etc.)
  2. Other things that may be important in the working environment
  3. Working conditions
  4. Co-workers
     a. desirable personal attributes
     b. undesirable personal attributes

B. Home environment
   1. Located near other ''specially selected'' people
   2. General type of dwelling
      a. Single family or apartment
      b. City, suburb, or country

After the exercise, each group reports its decisions. The faculty member then asks students to think about the decisions and about the process and asks them to analyze, individually, which elements of this ideal environment they were adamant about having. From this, students are encouraged to deduce what really matters to them, what they value, what should be factored in as they determine their goals.

By the time these activities are completed, students typically have a fair amount of insight into their dreams. Next the faculty member points out how to temper those dreams with the realities of their lives—how to look at their abilities, skills, and survival needs—and to create realistic goals and an action plan for accomplishing them. With this learning, students are able to draft the ''goal-setting'' paper that will be part of their portfolios.

After deciding on their life and career goals, students usually have the impetus to go through the rest of the CLLP process. Since they know what career they want, it is easier for them to determine what degree they should work toward and what course credits they need to receive it. With this knowledge, students are ready to move into the next phase of the course, articulating their experiential learning as it relates to Sinclair courses. This occurs during weeks four through nine.

As before, there is structure for students. During the fourth week of the term the instructor uses many examples on overhead transparencies to show students the difference between sentences that discuss experience and those that discuss learning. The faculty member also writes down on the chalkboard the experiences and learning of volunteers from the class and, with class participation, dissects their learning from their experience. It is also during this session that students begin discussing how to verify and document the learning. Here, discussion is vital. Frequently, a brainstorming session involving all class members identifies creative ways to document learning. Finally, the students are given another assignment. Since credit at Sinclair is awarded on a course-equivalent basis, students are asked to search through course descriptions in the Sinclair catalog to compare them with their learning experiences. They are then instructed to categorize this experiential learning and its relationship to Sinclair courses on the following worksheet.

	Taught at Sinclair— Required for Chosen Major	Taught at Sinclair— Not Needed for Major	No Sinclair Equivalent— Would Be Experiential Learning Elective Credit
Experience: participated in Toastmaster's Club	Speech 211		
Taught pre-schoolers in Vacation Bible		Child and Family 112	
Handled management of the family farm			Management Internship 270

In the fifth week of the term the instructor uses the class as a workshop session. Students bring the worksheet and, with the faculty member's help, use course syllabi and objectives to begin to compare and contrast their experiential learning with course content. Their assignment at the end of that session is to articulate their learning as it relates to at least one Sinclair course.

During the following weeks each student meets with the faculty member on one or more occasions to review and revise the developing portfolios of experiential learning and to discuss individual plans for documenting the learning. By the tenth week of the term, students have produced all the pieces of their portfolio and present the complete document for review.

Today's Credit for Lifelong Learning Program is grounded in a structured, classroom-based course in portfolio development. The group of adults in the course participates in activities designed to make the class sessions experiential, to allow the participants to discover their values, goals, self-worth, and, ultimately, the richness of their own learning. Students also learn how to extract learning from experience, and they take this new awareness of the potential for experiential learning with them into present and future experiences. They are far better equipped to be lifelong learners. Similarly, they leave the program with concrete life and career plans as well as increased skills both in setting goals and in testing those goals against reality.

Moreover, in addition to the predicted outcomes that many successful students share, our evaluation of the new design indicates still other, unanticipated outcomes. For instance, many students report that their portfolios were helping them get new jobs and promotions. One such student explained that she was one of five finalists for a promotion that she really wanted. As the only one of those finalists who did not have a baccalaureate degree, she felt that her chances of securing the new position were slim. Still, as a final resort, she gave her employer a copy of her recently completed portfolio and asked him to read it. In that document, she described not only her work history but her experiences and learning as a leader in her church for more than twenty years. She also recounted the learning she had acquired while helping her husband manage and operate a large farm with a complex record-keeping system. Several days later, her employer told her that until he read her portfolio he "never realized she had done so much." She got the new position.

Other students report increased self-esteem. One person explained that although he had a high-level executive position he had always felt uncomfortable about not having a degree, especially since many of his subordinates had graduate degrees. He described business lunches in which he would become silent or try to change the subject when a companion mentioned college. He was desperately embarrassed to admit that he had worked his way up without a degree. After completing a portfolio, his attitude changed. When he saw the finished document, he realized that he had learned as much as colleagues who had gone to college; he had just learned it differently. He discovered, as another student put it, that he could "look at the portfolio and say, 'Hey, I really have done something!' "

Another group of students found still another benefit in developing a portfolio. These students, all of whom were sixty-five or older, discovered that the finished portfolios made wonderful gifts for their families. One grandmother reported that her grandson appreciated receiving her life story—her portfolio—so much that he cried.

It became evident that earning college credits was only one outcome of the portfolio development process for many students. While they may have entered CLLP to earn college credits, other outcomes became more important than this original goal.

Both statistics and students' subjective feedback indicate that the objectives of the course are being met, as is the broader purpose of meeting the needs of the Sinclair adult population. Now, over 80 percent of the students who enroll in CLLP complete a portfolio, a 30 percent decrease in attrition. The comment of one student is more encouraging than any statistic. She wrote: "I would highly recommend this course to anyone starting or returning to college at age thirty-five or over even if there wasn't one competency that earned credit."

As described by Muriel Dance, the School of New Resources of the College of New Rochelle in New Rochelle, New York, frames prior learning assessment in a series of three courses taken at key stages in a student's education. Like CLLP at Sinclair Community College, these courses address career and life planning, but faculty have found that their students need a prior step. "While adults sometimes know a general career direction," says the author, "they ... are concerned about whether they can succeed in a college environment." The School of New Resources therefore begins the process with a "College Orientation" approach.

SCHOOL OF NEW RESOURCES, COLLEGE OF NEW ROCHELLE

Muriel Dance

The School of New Resources began in 1972 with the aims of recognizing that learning starts with the learner and of enabling adult students to be active participants in the design of their own education. Adults enrolling in the program in the early 1970s participated in the development of courses, sought credits for prior experiential learning through the development of a life experience portfolio, and earned credits through study in seminars and independent study—all with the emphasis on active participation in learning. There were no required courses. Students initiated requests for courses, which focused largely on issues of personal development and contemporary social problems.

The need for a formal approach to degree planning emerged as the school grew in size and as students and faculty alike identified the need for a more developed structure within which students could initiate course requests. Because of their significant role in determining the curriculum, students needed skills and a sense of purposefulness to participate effectively in the curriculum development process, which could only be as strong as their collective understanding of the issues and complexities of academic program design. Individually, too, students seemed to need a more formal approach. Because most intended to use their degrees to enhance an existing career or prepare for a new one, they needed to develop a more concrete sense of what they needed to study and how they should design their degrees.

In 1972 the students were primarily women living in the suburbs of lower Westchester and the employees of District Council 37, the municipal employees' union in New York City. Ethnically, most were Irish, Italians, African Americans, and Jews. Now, the students remain primarily women (79 percent), 84 percent of them from minority groups; the majority of the women are employed, single heads of household with two children, with a mean age of thirty-seven. These demographics belie the diversity of the school, however, which serves seven distinct communities within the metropolitan New York area.

This heterogeneous student body draws from diverse sources of prior experiential learning. While work proves to be the largest source of prior learning requests, usually in the human services and business fields, there are requests for recognition of learning gained completely outside of paid work experience. Other sources of prior experiential learning include community and volunteer activities that provide knowledge of public speaking, fund raising, and the theater. Within organizations, the church provides adults with skills in Sunday school teaching, while trade union activity is a source of prior learning at the D.C. 37 campus. Hobbies and independent reading are the other significant sources.

When the School of New Resources first decided to have students create a prior learning assessment portfolio in 1972, the document was intended to be an extended, reflective autobiographical essay. It was written later in a student's academic career and was seen as the culmination of an adults' baccalaureate experience, as a testimonial, often eloquent, to students' understanding of their own development. In 1982–83, New Resources changed several components of the program while maintaining its original philosophical aims. One of these changes involved a major revision of its approach to portfolio development, placing it within the framework of students' degree planning.

The rationale for linking degree planning and prior learning assessment grew out of a conviction that prior learning could best be identified after students knew enough about an academic program to translate experiential learning into course equivalents. Developmentally, this would encourage them to view the continuum between past and future learning. Further, it would allow them to explore their current skills in light of their career goals.

New Resources now requires its degree candidates to take specific courses at three curricular milestones: entrance (Experience, Learning, and Identity), midpoint (Career/Interest Review), and near completion (Designing the Future). These degree planning courses, referred to as ACCESS (Adult Career Counseling: Education and Support Services) courses, have three goals: (1) to provide students with the theoretical frameworks and information necessary to understand college, (2) to focus on the developmental needs of adults, and (3) to help adults plan individual courses of study. Thus, in addition to theoretical material, the seminars are developmental in approach.

New Resources found that few adults are ready to plan their courses of study or careers immediately upon entering college. A decision to enter college as an adult usually signals a life transition. While adults sometimes have a general career direction, they usually want an opportunity to explore, and they are concerned about whether they can succeed in a college environment. As part of its introduction to the liberal arts, Experience, Learning, and Identity focuses on what an adult needs to know about college: concepts and vocabulary, the nature of the disciplines, the various approaches to organizing curricula, the ways in which people learn. The seminar requires a great deal of reading, which alternates between autobiographies that help adults see the various ways people have learned and primary texts that introduce adults to the nature of the disciplines. Students read Plato's *Apology*, for example, but not as students in an introductory philosophy course. They are first asked to see similarities and differences between their own experiences and those described by Plato. They then move to the kinds of questions posed in the work and only then to an introduction to the kinds of questions asked by philosophy. At the end of the seminar students write their own educational autobiographies in which they describe significant learning experiences as well as goals for future learning. They are required to plan for at least one year of study, including how they will achieve the goals of general education, and if they are ready, they are encouraged to plan for the whole degree, identifying a concentration, possible prior experiential learning, and electives.

If the knowledge necessary for success in college is the theme of Experience, Learning, and Identity, then exploration career directions is the theme of the second milestone, Career/Interest Review. The educational autobiography is used again in an expanded form, but this time as material for adults to identify their own best transferrable career skills. In addition to identifying their best skills, students read from the career development literature, identify their own career values, and research career directions that would satisfy their values and use their best skills. The career direction is linked to the declaration of an area of interest and the refining of the degree plan to include a sequence of courses in the area of concentration. Students select from among five liberal arts areas offered by New Resources—psychology, social sciences, foreign languages, communications, and letters. The majority of students select psychology, probably because it relates closely to the two career objectives most commonly held by our students: education and social service. In addition, most students have a sequence of courses related to a career choice. While selecting a concentration, students make the decision to apply for credit for prior experiential learning, and the reading of the *Student Handbook on Preparation of a Prior Learning Portfolio* is an assignment in the course. At the end of their course, students have their degree plan approved by the academic staff of the campus.

The last milestone, Designing the Future, helps adults assess what they have accomplished in their degree and prepare for the transition to a better career, a new career, community service, or graduate school. Students read about the nature of work and its satisfactions and limitations, demonstrate their oral skills in videotaped interviews, demonstrate their writing skills by describing the rationale for their degree plan, highlight their skills and accomplishments by preparing professional resumes, and interview people who hold the positions to which they aspire.

Ideally, an adult registers for the school's Prior Learning Portfolio Workshop soon after the completion of Career/Interest Review, where most adults complete their first full degree plan. The workshop has five objectives: (1) to reexamine life/work experience for possible credit; (2) to review the standards for college-level learning and to understand New Resources' guidelines for the crediting of prior learning; (3) to examine the impact of possible prior learning credits on the degree plan; (4) to complete a draft of one area of learning, which includes a course description, a description of learning, a statement of competencies or learning outcomes achieved, and appropriate documentation; and (5) to prepare a detailed timetable for continuing work with a mentor on an individual basis until the portfolio is complete.

New Resources has identified six kinds of assessment methods: product assessment, performance assessment, oral interview, extended written work, essay or objective examination, and simulation. While each of these methods has been used, most evaluators prefer an oral interview or an examination when an additional assessment is needed. Each of these assessment modes has diagnosis as an aim.

In addition to recommending credit to be granted, an evaluator may recommend resources for strengthening an adult's experiential learning.

While closely linked to the three credit-bearing courses described above, the Prior Learning Portfolio Workshop carries no credit. It consists of four 2½ hour meetings between mentor and participants during the workshop and at least three individual meetings once the workshop has concluded. The typical workshop has five–eight students, although students can request permission to work with a mentor individually to achieve the workshop objectives.

During the four portfolio workshop meetings, usually held every other week, students sample portfolios that students before them have written. In addition to its pedagogical function, helping students identify the characteristics of college-level learning and providing a framework for completing a learning outline, this step both builds confidence and makes the project real. Students then present a significant life or work experience to other members of the workshop in order to minimize anxiety when they begin on their own and inevitably face a blank page.

The assignment following these first activities is the drafting of what we call a learning outline. The learning outline requires students to remember experiences that might be sources of college-level learning. These include paid employment, informal education, family/home management, volunteer work, recreation and hobbies, travel, and military service. Students are asked to estimate the time spent in the activity; to describe the tasks, activities, duties and training the experience involved; and to determine the skills, competences, knowledge gained as a result. Mentors have found that a skills list, such as that developed by the Junior League, helps to prod the memory when students fill out the learning outline.

For the second workshop session, students are helped to clarify their skills by reading aloud their learning outlines. Students often look again at finished portfolios in which students have made requests for credit similar to the ones they themselves plan. At this time students also compute the actual number of prior learning course requests they might ideally want to make. Students then draft one course request for the next meeting.

During the third session group reading of the drafts of course requests provides the focus. If, for example, a student describes roles and crises in his or her family and families close to the student, the class might point to courses in "Sociology of the Family" or "Families in Crisis'' as appropriate equivalents for credit, and the mentor might bring a syllabus for each of those courses to the workshop. The mentor stresses the function of a student's familiarity with appropriate vocabulary as a way of demonstrating to an evaluator that he or she has acquired the equivalent subject knowledge. Finally, the mentor asks students to identify possible ways to document the learning identified in their rough drafts.

The fourth and final session focuses on a discussion of documentation, different assessment modes, expectations for evaluation, and a reasonable process for completing the portfolio. Each student leaves the workshop with a follow-up appointment with the mentor. The portfolio must be completed and submitted within twelve months of the workshop and before the student has completed ninty credits. A maximum of thirty credits may be earned in this way.

The completion of the portfolio project affirms the linkages between prior learning assessment and degree planning in a number of ways. Because prior learning requests are included in the completed degree plan, on the practical level the two activities must be linked. To ensure that students themselves explore the connection, an introductory essay that relates prior learning to the course of study and to the student's life experience must be submitted as part of the portfolio.

As the School of New Resources looks more closely at outcomes of its graduates, we recognize that the level of skills and competence required by the portfolio process amply demonstrates general liberal arts competencies at the college level. In addition to obtaining credits through the portfolio, adults increase their sense of self-esteem and exercise their skills of critical thinking, writing, and planning. A recent survey of all graduates who had completed the portfolio program reaffirmed the multiple benefits for students in the portfolio process: as a result of completing the portfolio, 57 percent of the students reported a positive career change, 93 percent reported acceptance into and pursuit of a graduate degree, and 93 percent reported an enhanced self-concept.

The School for New Learning at DePaul University in Chicago offers a competency-based model of higher education to a largely business-oriented population of adult students. To help these students negotiate the return to school, the "Foundations of New Learning" course provides an intense exploration of liberal arts modes of thought and study. Thus, as author Betta LoSardo demonstrates, "Academic Skills" and "The Meaning of Education" become important components of a "College Orientation" approach.

The following essay is also important as the first of several discussions of assessment within competency-based programs. "In 'Foundations,'" says LoSardo, "students learn what the liberal arts are, not only in terms of the traditional content areas but also with relation to the problem-solving skills and creative thinking associated with liberal arts disciplines."

SCHOOL FOR NEW LEARNING, DEPAUL UNIVERSITY

Betta LoSardo

The School for New Learning (SNL) is DePaul University's nontraditional college for adults. Its student body, which has an average age of thirty-seven years, is 65 percent female and 20 percent minority. Most students live and work in the Chicago metropolitan area, but recent marketing efforts have expanded offerings at two suburban campuses that serve growing corporate centers.

SNL differs from many other alternative programs in that it does not grant credit for life experience on a course-equivalent basis. Rather, credit is awarded and curriculum built around a framework of competences. Competences differ from traditional academic organizations of knowledge in that they relate what students "know," to what they can "do" with that knowledge; thus, they help students define their experiences and relate to the larger problem-solving issues inherent in liberal arts study.

At SNL competences are grouped into five areas: lifelong learning, the arts of living, the human community, the physical world, and the world of work. These competences, numbering fifty, are designed to encompass liberal arts fields. Approximately three-fourths of these competences are standard components that all students must meet. Those remaining are designed individually by each student in conjunction with his or her advisory committee.

Although approximately 80 percent of SNL students focus their learning programs on business administration and related fields, there is very little homogeneity in students' curricular choices. For example, two students who select accounting as an area of concentration will exhibit differing course choices based on their levels of experience, current job requirements, and next considered career steps. Students also differ substantially in their familiarity with liberal arts requirements; in their writing, reading, reasoning, and research skills; and in their understanding of the rigor of university level work. Many, but by no means all, come to DePaul with some college experience. Approximately 20 percent have an associate's degrees; approximately 20 percent have no exposure to college work.

This diversity, in addition to SNL's student-centered philosophy, poses some interesting problems for the faculty member attempting to aid students in coordinating and presentating prior learning and in planning the balance of their degrees. As a result, all students who have evidenced secure, realizable career and academic goals are encouraged to enroll in the school's portfolio development and program design seminar, Foundations of New Learning. Early exposure to this course is particularly important for students who are especially attracted by the possibilities for assessment of experiential learning or who have done a great deal of previous college work.

Foundations is a nine-week course that offers six quarter hours of credit. Its design allows the instructor some flexibility with both content and scheduling. Many faculty members substitute individual counseling sessions for final class meetings or as a midterm check point. Much of the content of Foundations, however, is designed to elicit at group participation and indeed focuses on group dynamics and negotiation skills. The twenty-odd students who make up a particular Foundations group use one another as sounding boards in the process of developing academic skills and as preliminary evaluators for life experience projects. This give-and-take relationship prepares the student to direct his or her own learning process and reduces student reliance on faculty for "the right answer."

In addition to fostering academic independence and empowerment, Foundations has a number of objectives. First, its faculty has discovered that the student who understands that he or she is learning but who doesn't know how to organize and present that learning is extremely frustrated and is unlikely to complete the portfolio or degree program. Typically, students are baffled by the notion of credit for experiential learning and, lacking a context and methodology for self-evaluation, don't know where to begin. One major thrust of Foundations, therefore, is to show students how to identify, organize, evaluate, develop, and present learning.

Second, adult students often perceive themselves as disenfranchised. They aren't familiar with the standards of academe and don't know the vocabulary. Yet the School for New Learning will ask them to take charge of the educational process. Consequently the second objective of the Foundations course is to provide a backdrop, a guidebook to the "givens" of higher education. Ideally, each student walks away from the course with a concrete plan for achieving the B.A. degree, including specific methods and topics for each of the fifty competences.

Students arrive at Foundations asking two questions: What is this all about? How do I get credit for what I know? They are unfamiliar with the territory and usually on their way to other goals: an M.B.A., a law degree, a new career. The B.A. degree may be perceived as merely a stepping stone, a necessary evil. SNL tries to expand the breadth and vision of the answers to students' questions by structuring the course around four issues. These are What is learning? What are the liberal arts? What are college skills? How does experiential learning fit into the competence framework? Examination of these topics provides a college orientation that helps students place their knowledge, skills, and abilities within the broader context of human knowledge.

1. What is learning?

Students explore their learning styles and read selections from theories on adult learning. This step forms the foundation for understanding and planning their own learning skill development. It also provides students with an understanding of the type of education they are pursuing through SNL. Exposure to theoretical works in the field of alternative education helps students place the SNL program within the context of educational history and development. Specifically, students read, analyze, and discuss the ideas of such diverse theorists as John Dewey, David Kolb, Alfred North Whitehead, and George Klemp. Use of Dewey's statement on progressive schools in *Experience and Education* is a good example of SNL's emphasis on personalizing learning. As a "local" scholar at the University of Chicago, Dewey provided institutions and ideas that Chicagoans deal with on a daily basis. While Kolb and Klemp furnish the up-to-date analysis, the selection from Whitehead's *The Aims of Education* gives students access to the historical perspective.

2. What are the liberal arts?

Students tend to define a liberal arts education by what it is *not*, that is, it is not a business degree, nor it is a Bachelor of Science. In Foundations students learn what the liberal arts *are*, not only in terms of the traditional content areas but also in with relation to the problem-solving skills and creative thinking that are associated with liberal arts disciplines. Students who expect to design a competence-based liberal arts B.A. must have a clear idea of the interrelation of these fields and how the interrelation shapes the whole.

In Foundations students discover, for example, that the study of environmental issues does not fall solely in the province of the natural sciences. It also is influenced by social, historical, and philosophical concerns. Thus, students might read excerpts from Rachel Carson's *Silent Spring* or an essay on environmentally caused illnesses. One student, whose family operates a refrigerator distributorship, contributed an oral presentation on population growth and the demand for freon.

An in-class exercise demonstrates the critical thinking and self-reliance fostered in the course. The exercise has two purposes: to introduce the kinds of questions and methods surrounding liberal arts inquiry and to encourage students to participate in group negotiation.

Students are asked to define and rank the following seven statements, which describe liberal arts problem solving.

- Ask the right questions.
- Be conscious of your values.
- Communicate with precision.
- Find relevant information.
- Make wise decisions.
- Think in a logical, disciplined manner.
- Understand the culture.

By design, no specific content is assigned to these questions. Students must place the question within their own framework and explain their understanding of each area to other group members.

Beginning SNL students, schooled in the teacher-knows-the-answer philosophy of previous educational experiences, sometimes find it difficult to develop their own topics and standards. This exercise fosters comfort with the idea of creating one's own context and arguing it through. Faculty members serve as observers and facilitators for those students who find the task overwhelming.

3. What are college skills?

Foundations forces students to look critically at their preparedness to achieve their goals. To give faculty and students a starting point, specific testing in writing and reasoning is administered before the course begins. Through these exercises and faculty feedback, students discover their strengths and weaknesses. The faculty stresses the importance of these learning skills both to the immediate issues of portfolio development and to the eventual completion of the B.A. degree.

Students complete a reading analysis worksheet for each of approximately fifteen readings dispersed through the course. These articles cover a variety of topics, which correspond to the five areas of the SNL competence framework. They include several writing styles and represent authors whose works span several centuries. All materials are presented in the spirit of discovery. Thus, students might read from Georgio Vasari's *Lives of the Artists* and from Stanislau Lem. They might also hear from authors on computer technology and medical ethics.

Questions on the worksheets have students cover a wide range, from naming an article's thesis and explaining how various arguments support the thesis to analyzing the article's title, trying to decipher the author's intended audience, and relating each reading to course objectives.

The reading analysis worksheets serve as a checkpoint for faculty evaluation of students' reading and reasoning skills. The readings themselves help familiarize students with the content and contexts of liberal arts learning. In addition, the worksheets give them a means for self-evaluation. The faculty focuses class discussion on worksheet questions and on the relevance of particular readings to the students' lives and educational plans.

4. How does experiential learning fit into the competence framework?

Of necessity, some time is spent in Foundations on the forms and procedures of prior learning assessment and the details of applying accredited experiential learning toward a degree. More important, however, students are given a perspective from which to see their learning as part of a larger system of knowledge. The Foundations student examines aspects of his or her experience in supervision, for example, that might demonstrate skills in applied psychology. Similarly, another student might look at the sociological underpinnings of community development volunteer work.

Thus, in addition to appreciating the learning they have already acquired, students develop a view of the experientially enriching effect that classroom learning and skill development can have on their jobs, families, and leisure time. This notion helps the students over the rough spots when some valued life experience does not fit into the competence framework and new learning is required.

The experiential learning exercise is generally conducted on the first night of class. Its purpose is to get people thinking analytically about their experiences. Students use this exercise as the basis for a preliminary essay exploring an aspect of their experiential learning. Later they will apply that learning to the competence framework and evaluate it in greater depth.

The exercise utilizes the model presented in David Kolb's learning cycle. First, students must identify and define an experience from which they have learned. Recalling detail is important at this stage. Next, students describe their observations and reactions to the experience. The faculty points out that there is a difference between acknowledging that an observation exists and writing it down for others to appreciate. Students are encouraged to explore the manner in which thoughts are internalized. The third stage of Kolb's cycle requires that students articulate theories by identifying concepts or generalizations to be drawn from the experience and observations. Finally, to complete the cycle, students discuss how to test this new information and use it for new experiences.

This exercise helps Foundations participants locate the fine line between having an experience, or experience in general, and learning from it. Students analyze not only the facts but also their reactions to an experience, their assumptions, and their speculations. They can temper this information with additional research. This is particularly helpful when an experience is related to a competence, but does not directly address it.

The largest difficulty students face is the actual identification of experience appropriate to the SNL competence framework. Students and faculty work together to discuss potentialities and their ''fit'' with specific competences. Thus, the student who worked on a political campaign may have learned about motivation theories or about the way politics shapes history. As part of their work, therefore, students examine specific competences and try to find appropriate matches between theory and practice.

Once completed, students' prior learning projects are submitted to a Foundations faculty member who reviews them and then submits them to a central assessment committee chaired by SNR's assessment coordinator and made up of other Foundations faculty. External evaluations are also available from SNL and DePaul faculties.

A battle continues to rage at SNL over whether to provide students with examples of fulfilled competences. One side of the argument is the notion that students want and need direction. Some staff maintain that direction may stifle creativity and self-reliance. Nonetheless, each student is provided with a sample program and some actual approved documents. Faculty members emphasize the individualized nature of SNL while discussing these in class.

SNL academic staff are profoundly aware that developing a prior learning portfolio is not a simple matter. Identifying an experience appropriate to a specific competence is in itself a difficult task. The Foundations course provides a nonthreatening forum for explanation of the competences and examination of sample relevant experiences. As faculty often states in class, however, it's not the experience that earns the credit, it's the learning itself. Through David Kolb's theories of experiential learning, adapted for use in the SNL program, Foundations students analyze the content of learning experiences, the process of acquiring knowledge, and the demonstration of learning for the competence in question.

This process is followed for every competence achieved at SNL. The student must understand the content and value of prior learning, be it course work from a previous institution, a management seminar, or a lifelong interest in Eskimo arts. This experience also hones the student's understanding of the relationship of an individual learning experience to the entirety of the B.A. degree and to the reality of lifelong learning.

The competence framework lends itself more to the analysis of the interrelationship of ideas than to the repeating of facts. Students thus find it difficult to find a place in the framework for simple factual knowledge. CLEP and other content testing, while acceptable for credit at SNL, are not the preferred method of evidencing prior learning. Students discover that they must work through why this information is useful to them and what conclusion they reached as a result of their new knowledge. This is also true of another method of evidence, the letter of testimony. So, the student who is fluent in a language other than English must make a case for the relationship of his or her knowledge to understanding how a foreign culture works. Similarly, the student who is an expert painter must discuss the medium and defend it as an art form.

The Foundations of New Learning course attempts to foster in the SNL student the idea that self-direction and responsibility are the hallmarks of the educated person and the keys to success at the School for New Learning. Requirements, standards, and methods are made accessible through continual discussion and clarification. Faculty members serve as facilitators, as advisors, as evaluators, in essence, as bridges to learning. Students thrive in the supportive but challenging atmosphere fostered in the course and gradually become comfortable within the less structured environment of nontraditional education and lifelong learning.

The Assessment of Prior Learning Program is an important component of The American University's commitment to serving the diverse community of Washington, D.C. Preceded by a reading and writing course on social and personal analysis, the portfolio development seminar takes a multicultural, socially interactive approach to the theme of "Personal Exploration." Readings and discussions help students "reflect on their life experiences," explains author Richard Roughton, "and develop a broader theoretical understanding that includes the role of gender, race, and culture in their own development as human beings."

THE OFFICE OF CONTINUING STUDIES, THE AMERICAN UNIVERSITY

Richard Roughton

The American University in Washington, D.C., grants baccalaureate, master's, and doctoral degrees and is currently serving over 11,000 students. Approximately 5,000 of these students are undergraduates, some fifth of whom study part-time. This last group of part-time undergraduates consists largely of adults over the age of twenty-five, and the Assessment of Prior Learning Program (APEL) is one aspect of the university explicitly designed to serve them.

Students typically come to the APEL program after a long period of reflection, in which fears and self-doubts about their ability to succeed in the program are weighed against the gains a degree can provide. Many adults do not automatically make the connection between learning and experience and thus feel far removed from educational attainment. Further, many have negative feelings about earlier experiences of schooling; memories of bad grades, boredom, poor teachers, and more further discourage a return to school.

APEL, like many such programs, uses the process of prior learning assessment to help students see the connection between classroom education and experiential learning. In so doing, it seeks to fulfill two related goals. First, prior learning assessment typically helps experienced adults with the practical matters of degree completion; at the same time, it encourages them to approach education as a lifelong project.

In addition to its general commitment to serving adult learners is the university's commitment to increasing the ethnic diversity of the student body; as a predominantly white institution in a city in which whites are a minority, this commitment is an important aspect of our ability to serve Washington as a whole. The success of the APEL program thus depends in no small part on its ability to serve the African American, Asian American, and Latino communities in the area. Through its Office of Continuing Studies, the university uses prior learning assessment as a way to reach out to these communities.

The university is proud of its success in meeting this objective. Over 30 percent of APEL students are from underrepresented communities within academe, while faculty and staff also come from all the communities we serve. In addition, the two required courses in the program use texts and other materials that reflect the experiences of women and of Latino, Asian, and African American cultures.

APEL structures its program for adults into a four-stage process: orientation and admission; our entry course, Issues, Ideas, and Words; the portfolio seminar; and course work leading to degree completion. The integration of students into APEL's approach thus begins even before admission, in the outreach and orientation process itself. A variety of university outreach efforts that announce orientation sessions are targeted to the adult audience. Orientation sessions allow prospective students to talk with staff and alumni about the linkages between experiential and classroom learning in a program that includes prior learning assessment. After orientation, prospective students meet individually with academic advisors who have been trained to evaluate adult students for the APEL program. The interviews last one hour and include discussion of the student's goals and a preliminary examination of assessment possibilities. Thus the student is encouraged from the outset to link education back to prior learning and ahead to goals for the future.

After registration, students enter the course, Issues, Ideas, and Words, developed by the Literature Department in collaboration with the Office of Continuing Studies. Its goals were perhaps best articulated by the faculty member who first taught it in 1978: "to introduce (or reintroduce) you to academic work, to the investigation of ideas, to intellectual play, and to the appreciation of ideological heresy." These goals are realized through attention to "generating an interest in ideas for their own sake" but also through "cultivat[ing] a critical attitude about the words that express them." Importantly, the critical attitude toward words goes beyond the development of reading skills to address weaknesses in students' own writing.

Experience has shown that the course is a useful introduction or reintroduction to the world of college work. Limited to groups of no more than fifteen returning students, it is for many their their first academic experience in years; it is for others an introduction to the standards and expectations of The American University. For all, it is an ice-breaker that also can also be applied toward the university's English requirement.

Rather than mandating a particular set of readings and assignments, the Issues, Ideas, and Words syllabus structures general guidelines from which individual courses are built. Typically, each class reads four or five books, including an anthology of shorter readings and at least one autobiography, novel, and book on contemporary issues. In keeping with the multicultural orientation of the program, at least one book in each class is by a woman and at least one by a person of color.

In addition to being focal points for writing and class discussion, the readings are vehicles to help students learn to critique texts. We have found that the variety of genres helps students learn to analyze different kinds of writing. Students are also required to work on their own with a writing handbook. Simultaneously, most students take advantage of the various support services the university offers adults. Workshops and seminars are readily available on study skills, time and stress management, critical reading, writing, and other topics.

Most faculty members choose to organize the reading and writing assignments to reflect a theme or to develop students' abilities to critique literary texts. The faculty often chooses an issue that connects important literary texts with contemporary social issues. Thus, instructors have developed course syllabi around "crime and punishment," in which the Dostoevsky novel is the main text, and "technology in modern society," using Herbert Butterfield's *Scientific Revolution* as the focus. Autobiographies commonly selected include Maxine Hong Kingston's *The Woman Warrior* and Nien Chang's *Life and Death in Shanghai*. The link between literary texts and contemporary social issues is an important one, for the course is meant as a path from the world of experience to the academic world and, in fact, is a prerequisite to the portfolio development course.

This two-step process, in which students complete the Issues course before enrolling in the portfolio seminar, helps ensure that students come to portfolio development with the skills they will need. In giving them the opportunity to develop their ability to read critically and, particularly, write effectively, the Issues course helps prepare many students for the substantial task of preparing a portfolio. The course also requires students to work with the medium of autobiography. Initially they read and evaluate autobiographical texts, discuss the reading in class, and write five-page papers analyzing the reflective processes at work in the text. They then refine their own reflective process by writing their own autobiographies. The placement of the autobiographical writing assignment toward the end of the course provides an excellent bridge to the portfolio seminar.

The portfolio seminar is a three-credit course that takes a multicultural approach to the theme of adult development. The course is designed to help adult students meet a number of objectives. First, it allows them to acquire an understanding of some contemporary theories of adult learning and development that will be useful to them in a higher education setting. Second, it helps them identify, analyze, and synthesize prior experiential learning, the final product being the portfolio that articulates and documents that learning. Third, it enhances their existing academic and planning skills and helps them acquire new ones. Finally, it promotes their understanding of and adaption to the goals and culture of higher education, with particular attention paid to those of The American University.

Readings presented during the first five weeks of the course inform the portfolio development process by offering both developmental theory and case studies. Discussions of the readings help students reflect on their life experiences and develop a broader theoretical understanding that includes the role of gender, race, and culture in their own development as human beings. As students draw closer to portfolio writing, they are led to explore their lives as a developmental process. To help them accomplish this goal, the faculty uses a set of readings that guides students toward greater levels of insight into their own development.

These readings include "A Conception of Adult Development" by Daniel J. Levinson, "Concepts of Self and Morality" from *In a Different Voice* by Carol Gilligan, and "Understanding Adults' Life and Learning" from *Improving Higher Education Environments for Adults* by Nancy Schlossberg, Arthur Chickering, and Ann Q. Lynch. These three assignments are given early in the course and set the stage for what is often animated discussion of students' own adult development. At this stage in the course, students take the Strong-Campbell Interest Inventory and revise their autobiographies. Initially assigned to help students improve their writing style, the autobiography is now recast with the goal of helping them gain greater insight into their developmental process.

In the next stage of the course, students identify the fields that will be included in their portfolios and quickly proceed to write their first portfolio component. The texts assigned to assist them are Susan Simosko's *Earn Credits for What You Know* and Peter Elbow's *Writing without Teachers*. Students also consult with the faculty members who will evaluate and assign credit for each component. These discussions encourage students to see their experience in relationship to academic fields as they are taught at the university.

As students work more and more intently on their portfolios, class discussion continues to focus on informing the developmental process. Readings at this stage include Charles S. Claxton and Patricia H. Murrell, "Learning Styles: Implications for Improving Educational Practices" and Parker Palmer's "Community Conflict and Ways of Knowing." There is often some resistance to continued reading assignments, as students focus increasingly on the hard work of writing the portfolio. The faculty believes strongly, however, that the readings help students better understand the portfolio development process, and faculty meetings continue to explore ways to help students better understand the connections between the readings and the writing of strong portfolios.

Students take much pride in their completed portfolios. When they receive their credit awards there is a strong sense of accomplishment, accompanied by a great sigh of relief. At the same time students are aware that the experience has united varied forms of learning and can see the rest of formal education not simply as unfinished business but as another step in a process that has spanned their lives.

APEL's success is rooted in its ability to encourage returning adults to see their education historically. School is no longer seen as intrusive but as part of a larger learning context that can shape lifelong goals and objectives. Some students chose to pursue degrees in fields such as management, with career promotions as their major goals. Others favor humanities degrees, deciding that intellectual challenge means more to them than practical concerns. In either case, they have had an opportunity to integrate worklife skills and knowledge with a strong academic base and to experience the connections between the traditional subject matter of academe and their social and personal experience of the world.

The following essay, on the Educational Assessment and Portfolio Preparation course offered by the Office of External Programs of the Vermont State Colleges, is the first of two models of an "Academic Skills" approach. In this model, author Dee Steffans argues that portfolio development provides the opportunity to hone critical thinking and communication skills and to gain experience with academic categories and modes of inquiry. The program, says Steffans, has a second major objective in addition to the assessment itself; namely, "to incorporate methodologies that draw out and enhance the student's ability to think conceptually and analytically."

The portfolio development course is also important as an example of a centralized, noninstitutionally based program that serves a number of schools in a region. Centralization and coordination of this service among colleges within a region or state system is an important option that was pioneered by the Vermont system. Further, the shared program promotes common standards of assessment across neighboring institutions and avoids the implicit competition for students among institutions that assess prior learning.

OFFICE OF EXTERNAL PROGRAMS, VERMONT STATE COLLEGES

Dee Steffans

For the past twelve years the Vermont State Colleges Office of External Programs has administered one of the largest and most successful programs in the country for the assessment of prior learning. It is a statewide, noninstitutionally based program awarding Vermont State Colleges transfer credit to hundreds of adults each year. Since its inception in 1976 this program has assisted over 2,500 adults in beginning or returning to college.

The Vermont State Colleges system comprises the state's five public colleges; the Assessment of Prior Learning program operates out of the Office of External Programs (OEP), which is the research and development arm of the state colleges system. Most of the programs OEP develops and supports are made available to all of the state colleges, and the assessment program is no exception. Educational Assessment and Portfolio Preparation (EAPP), the fifteen-week course developed by OEP and required of all assessment applicants, is offered at four of the five state colleges, through several colleges outside the system, and through outside agencies or organizations in Vermont. Because OEP is not affiliated with any one college or university, students can enroll through any sponsoring site and transfer to any institution of higher education that accepts experiential learning credits. The credits awarded are considered VSC-OEP *transfer* credits, and receiving institutions make final determinations about which credits they will accept.

Demographic surveys show that about 75 percent of our students are women, most are in their thirties and fourties and two thirds employed full-time. Seventy percent come to assessment with some college background; of those, most have had less than one year of college education. At present we are seeing a shift in background from education and social services to business. In the past year fully half of our portfolios were in business areas, including administration, management, and sales. Other major areas of concentration include computers, education, human services, health fields, and technology. Students can request credit in any subject as long as the learning is college level. Thus, we see some unorthodox requests in areas not typically found in a Vermont college catalog, such as equine studies, subsistence fishing, fire sciences, home schooling curriculum design, and community organizing.

There are no prerequisites for EAPP. Experience has taught us, however, that students should be old enough to have acquired significant experiential learning and should have good writing skills. Advisors often suggest that students take English composition prior to enrolling. Because EAPP is one of the more demanding courses available to students, we also advise that they take no other courses during the semester and that they enlist the support (physical and psychological) of family and friends while enrolled.

Since beginning to assess prior learning twelve years ago, we have been driven in our programmatic development by two major objectives: to provide a process that accurately and thoroughly reflects each student's extrainstitutional college-level learning and to incorporate methodologies that elicit and enhance the student's ability to think conceptually and analytically. The first objective reflects an orientation toward product, namely, the portfolio. The finished document is evaluated in light of its presentation, its content, and the strength of verification by qualified documenters; the quality of the product influences the outcome of the evaluation.

But the course is far from being simply product oriented. When students examine their experiential learning for knowledge that is college level, they undertake a process that introduces them to the rigors of academic inquiry itself. Their own experience serves as a vehicle by which they further develop and hone critical thinking skills. They must categorize, organize, assess, and evaluate their learning to determine its applicability to and comparability with college-level learning. As a means to that end, students gain exposure to or practice in degree planning, programmed writing instruction, conceptual skill development, problem solving, learning theory discussion, interpersonal and group communication skill building, and an overview of the higher education system.

In keeping with the principles of good assessment practice, we maintain a strict emphasis on *learning* and not experience. Students must extract the learning derived from life experience and articulate it in a manner that facilitates an accurate assessment. They are challenged to assess their own learning as a preliminary step in the process, as they learn to distinguish between creditable, college-level learning and all other learning they have derived from experience. Here conceptual and analytical thinking skills can spell the difference between success and failure for students, and so substantial effort is invested in developing those modes of thought.

Of equal importance is the ability to articulate at the college level. Thinking and writing are treated as integrally connected processes; writing becomes the tool by which students draw conclusions, test hypotheses, evaluate the soundness of their arguments, and identify and raise new questions for inquiry. The subject of their writing varies, but the focus on learning and knowledge remains. On one level, students are developing skills to put together a successful portfolio. On another, more far-reaching level, they are adjusting to academic modes of inquiry and academic categorizations of thought: they are making sense of their world, and of their place in time.

It has become clear that the emotional and intellectual rigors of the assessment course produce results less tangible, though no less valuable, than college credits. Over and over our students credit the assessment course for its role in helping them to develop and hone skills necessary for success in subsequent studies. As an additional outcome, they cite an increased sense of self-confidence, self-worth, and personal insight.

Educational Assessment and Portfolio Preparation opens with an overview of the course. Instructors provide a syllabus and their expectations for successful completion. Following a warm-up exercise designed to introduce class members, instructors can select from a variety of writing projects to loosen the pens and inhibitions of the group.

Because EAPP is so heavily oriented toward writing, we start right in with regular writing exercises. The first activity, an easy and non-threatening assignment in free association, provides the instructor with a writing sample from each student. Students are asked to free write a spontaneous monolog, without regard for form or grammar. Over the course of the next fourteen weeks the nature of the writing assignments becomes more complex and more directly relevant to the final product, the portfolio. An underlying objective is to steer students toward more academic modes of discourse, since their abilities to make connections, to generalize from the specific, and to use precise, accurate language are considered essential for success in academe.

In the first five weeks students are asked to write about significant learning experiences, influential teachers, and step-by-step learning processes. One objective is to bring them an appreciation of the difference between experience and learning; another is to foster a greater understanding of the nature of learning itself. Students develop exhaustive lists of experiences they've had since high school—jobs, classes, milestone events such as marriage and childbirth. During the third week instructors begin to shift the emphasis from experience to learning. Bloom's *Taxonomy* is introduced as students practice making the distinction between action verbs and verbs that express learning or knowledge. To prepare for the narrative essay, students engage in writing activities that help to develop a focused and fluid style. Many instructors encourage students to keep a daily journal as a means of building confidence in their ability to write and familiarity with the writing process. Ultimately, each student works through three or four drafts of the essay, which averages eight–fifteen pages.

The next several weeks prove the most challenging for the majority of assessment students. Through group exercises and class discussion, students gain practice in extracting learning from experience and in articulating their knowledge in the form of short, concise learning statements. Eventually they begin to organize those statements into related ''areas of study,'' which later compose the substance of a ''summary transcript.''

The concepts presented at this point are difficult, and students progress in their understanding at varying rates. We usually find that frustrations peak at about the fifth week, when the nature of the required task becomes clear but the methodology for successful implementation seems vague and overwhelming. Students grapple with the articulation of learning for four concentrated weeks. At this point, a representative from OEP visits each class to review the first quarter of the course and to reinforce lessons on Bloom's verbs.

It is also during the fifth week that a new and critical concept is introduced: college-level learning. In developing their portfolios students reflect deeply on past experiences, not simply to recount and record what was learned but to apply it within the context of the portfolio. Once the learning has been identified, detailed, and organized into related areas of study, students must determine if and how their knowledge relates to learning that is typically credited at the college level. This is the heart of the process and its most difficult aspect.

At this point the student is presented with criteria for what makes learning college level. While this concept can cause consternation and is at times nebulous, it is not arbitrary. OEP has identified certain principles of learning that when taken together suggest that learning has earned the stamp of "college level." Our approach to establishing standards is both historical and abstract. We consider what colleges have traditionally taught and isolate bodies of knowledge common to higher education. We then examine the content within these disciplines to "abstract" principles that seem to define college-level quality.

To be credited, a student's learning must evidence the following qualities: it must be describable in words, have general applicability outside the context in which it was learned, relate to traditional academic disciplines, contain both theoretical and applied components, represent learning that transcends what is "common to all," and be verifiable. We ask students to hold their learning to these standards and subsequently discard for consideration any learning that fails to meet the criteria. Documentation is a critical piece of the portfolio. Each credit request must be accompanied by supporting primary documentation— letters verifying learning for which credit has been petitioned. These letters must be written directly to OEP by past or present associates with first-hand knowledge of a student's learning. Generally, documenters are supervisors, teachers, or experts in a field relevant to the area of request. Demands placed upon documenters are high in terms of the time and thoughtfulness required to produce a good piece of documentation. Often documenters have a professional relationship with students; sometimes they do not. Whichever is the case, the focus of the letter must be on learning that the student has demonstrated, usually in the context of the learning components articulated in the summary transcript.

As the semester progresses, students continue to work individually, in small groups, and as a class to perfect each section of the portfolio. The second half of the course is spent developing a degree plan; a resume of past work, volunteer, and educational experiences; and a bibliography of relevant readings. Structured activities include a mock advanced-standing committee exercise (in which students act as evaluators and assess a sample portfolio), a college night (attended by representatives from colleges around the state who talk about their programs), and a second visit from OEP during the tenth week. In the final weeks of the course students work primarily one-on-one with instructors to polish their portfolios and tie up loose ends. By the fifteenth week, if the process is successful, a transformation is taking place. Students feel a sense of closure about their past learning, because they have defined and, to some extent, quantified it for themselves. They shift their focus forward to the learning that awaits them, better prepared to integrate the new and the old by virtue of their comprehensive, methodical look back.

We have found that EAPP benefits everyone who takes part. Students clearly gain from a program that credits them for learning they've mastered. In the process of identifying, organizing, and describing what they know, they acquire skills that will better prepare them for what lies ahead in the college classroom. No less important, students fortify themselves for the challenge in undertaking a process that leads to increased self-confidence and self-esteem.

The educational institutions of Vermont have grown because of EAPP as well. In 1984 OEP conducted a survey that revealed an increase in adult enrollments directly attributable to the availability of prior learning assessment. More than one third of alumni responded that without the program they would probably not have pursued degrees. Less measurable, but still significant, is the understanding and responsiveness to the needs of adult students that prior learning assessment provides. Education across the Vermont State Colleges system benefits from a program that pushes all those involved to analyze and integrate the many ways adults learn. In Vermont the concept and the process of prior learning assessment have worked well for many years, and we look forward to a bright and promising future.

The second version of the "Academic Skills" approach, used by the University Without Walls of the University of Massachusetts, Amherst, focuses on writing about experience. According to author Gail Hall, having students write case studies of their own experience, autobiographical reflections on their sense of identity, and articulations of professional principles allows them to explore the dimensions of prior learning where it is most utilized: in the decision-making process itself. That process, in addition to producing viable portfolios of prior learning, serves as an effective mechanism for honing academic skills. "The case study," says Hall, "describes how a problem is solved but also makes a point about the particular profession or field involved." When complicated and subtle situations are analyzed, experiential learning is displayed and writing skills are developed.

UNIVERSITY WITHOUT WALLS, UNIVERSITY OF MASSACHUSETTS, AMHERST

Gail A. Hall

In 1972 the Commonwealth of Massachusetts gave the vote for president to George McGovern and its university gave the green light to a number of campus-based liberal experiments. One of these, the University Without Walls (UWW), was charged to open the doors of the university to those who were eager to learn but who had been excluded because of discrimination, logistics, or other reasons. A staff of four, mostly working part-time, set up an office in an old farm house on the edge of campus. We sought students who were intelligent and skilled and whose accomplishments we respected, but who were outsiders, students for whom college was both attractive and mysterious. At the same time we sought to stretch the boundaries of the campus to include new places to learn: work, home, the artist's studio, the streets. Armed with grant money from the Ford Foundation and the United States Office of Education, the enthusiasm of the university's best faculty, and the strength of our students, we set out to make a university education available to all. As part of our mandate, we started designing a process for crediting what our "outsider" students had learned from the world of work.

For about five years, we drove Commonwealth of Massachusetts Dodge Darts all over the state, teaching introductory-level college courses to students whose determination to succeed against terrible odds humbled and exhilarated us. We taught different courses in different semesters, depending on who needed what to satisfy university "core" requirements. But something was missing. With a deliberately diverse student body taking different courses, designing degrees in a range of fields at five separate sites, and writing their prior learning portfolios primarily on their own, the program had become fragmented, both for students and staff. In an effort to provide coherence, as well as sanity, we developed what has come to be the UWW curriculum.

It was in many ways the seriousness with which we took the task of individualizing degrees that led us to standardize a small portion of each student's program. It was important to prepare students well for the work of designing a degree, particularly given the setting in which this task took place. UWW is a program with its own ideas, but it is also a response to the strengths and idiosyncrasies of the institution that hosts it. I tell my students that UMass is the Filene's basement of higher education. Though courses are sometimes offered in buildings where the ceilings drip and fluorescent lights flicker, they are taught by nationally known scholars and the finest teachers money can buy. While the quality is high, however, getting at what you want can be a challenge. One of the biggest challenges is scheduling: few courses are offered at night. To complete an existing major, students cannot hold full-time jobs. Necessity being a good mother, we have invented a fine alternative to the majors on the books at UMass. Starting with an average of fifty transfer credits (the limit is seventy-five), students create interdisciplinary areas of concentration using those courses offered at night, additional transfer credit for courses offered at neighboring institutions, and day courses that they attend by using vacation time or by cutting back work hours, until the coveted degree is earned. In addition to classroom courses, they pursue independent projects, including the prior learning portfolio, with faculty who donate time to the UWW program above and beyond their departmental duties. The university's best faculty work with UWW because they care about teaching, because adults are interesting, because our students talk them into it. While we can't depend on any one department to deliver everything our students need, we can depend on the sheer size and variety offered by a university with 1,200 faculty members.

One of the primary goals of the few core courses now standardized in the curriculum was to unleash the learning potential inherent in the life experience of adults. In his book-length autobiographical poem, *Another Life*, Derek Walcott says, "A man lives half of life, the second half is memory."[1] For adults, going back to school is not only a way to plan for the future but a way to make sense of the past. Trying to figure out what happened in their lives is a task all adults spend more time on than they are likely to admit. Picking up on this flow of energy and building it into the curriculum, as those who work with adult students know only too well, is more than a curricular convenience; it is an organizing principle that allows students not only to deepen their understanding of their experience but to gain the confidence to move on and study new and totally unrelated subjects. In short, we believe that coming to understand the past is liberating.

UWW offers a curriculum that attempts to provide a common intellectual starting point for college study along with the individualized attention that helps students understand what is being asked of them both educationally and bureaucratically. Toward this end we combine individual advising with a core of three courses. Students take two of them, Perspectives on Learning and Degree Development Seminar during their first semester. Writing about Experience, the UWW portfolio development course, follows.

Perspectives on Learning is designed to introduce students to the effect experience has on the way they see the world. We use readings, films, and discussion to help them begin to appreciate how our culture, with its unspoken assumptions and beliefs, filters what we see and hear and influences our thinking. We believe a successful lifelong learner benefits from knowing how the identity acquired as a member of a family, or by reason of gender, racial, or ethnic grouping, provides both a solid starting point for understanding the world and, ironically, a set of blinders that can hinder that understanding.

The syllabus for this course distills the best ideas from the writing, literature, and social science courses taught in the early years of the program. Over time, we have come to believe that students can apprehend the power of cultural forces most quickly when they observe their effect on individuals with whom they can identify, at least in part. We ask them to read *The Woman Warrior* by Maxine Hong Kingston and *The Chaneysville Incident* by David Bradley, the former

---

[1]*Derek Walcott*, Another Life *(Washington, D.C.: Three Continents Press, 1973), 97.*

an autobiographical and the latter a fictional account of individuals caught between two cultures. These individuals struggle to understand the cultures in which their families have existed so they can see who they have become. We introduce these works after assigning some initial readings on the concept of culture along with other short pieces of autobiography and fiction that further suggest connections among individual identity, family experience, and education.

The writing assignments for the course are designed to move students along a continuum. We begin with accounts of personal experience. We might ask students to identify the ways in which the values of their families were passed on to them: "In what way was language or ritual used to bind members of your family? How do the language or ritual practices in your family compare with the mechanisms we find in our readings?" The second and third writing assignments move personal experience from the foreground to the background, and students are asked to engage more directly with the text. But the questions we ask again pinpoint the connection of culture to individual in the struggle to derive meaning from experience. We might ask, for instance, why the mother in *The Woman Warrior* is a hero in China but seems to be, at least to some extent, a frustrated tyrant in America. Where does the difference lie? In the mother, in the cultures in which she existed, or in the mind of the daughter/storyteller? With an assignment such as this students are asked to perform a thinking and writing task they will face again in other courses, specifically, formulating and defending a thesis. In this way we are able to prepare students for success in academic study by equipping them with traditional tools, but we also challenge the preexisting ideas they may have about where their thinking originates.

In the companion first semester course, Degree Development Seminar, students develop a plan for their studies. They begin by identifying what they as individuals wish to acquire in the way of skills and knowledge to prepare themselves for the future. For instance, a computer programmer may write that experience in a variety of jobs has led to a desire to work with computers and help nonprofit organizations meet the demands of the information age. Such a student may have come to UWW to prepare for a specific job, but after further thought and some coaching from the instructor might decide to broaden the focus and design a degree in public administration. The next step is to complete a research project on the history, current status, and future of the chosen field. To further promote a balance of professional studies with liberal arts, this student will use the library to investigate the field of public administration itself. Where did the field of public administration come from? Where is it going? What effect does it have on the society in which it exists? What effect does the society have on the work of public administrators? To get a better understanding of trends and issues as well as specific advice on what courses to take, the student will be asked to interview both faculty members who teach in the field and professionals outside the university. The final step in the process is to distill this new perspective into a degree proposal.

Once the above courses are completed, by the second or third semester, students complete Writing about Experience, the UWW portfolio preparation course. Within the program different instructors have developed different aspects of the course, but all share a common goal: to help students uncover the themes and issues that give meaning to professional practice.

In some ways, Writing about Experience, which meets the university's junior year writing requirement, looks a lot like other writing courses of the current period. We use two thirds of each class for peer editing. A five-ten page paper is due nearly every week. In the first half of the semester students write first drafts; in the second half, revisions. But in other ways, the course is very different. Our subject is problem solving. The task is not simply to describe experience but to reframe the past as a series of problems and solutions that have determined the writer's point of view about a particular kind of work.

The design of the portfolio course has been through several metamorphoses. Originally we saw the portfolio process as a teaching tool, but we were also looking for a short cut, a fast way to get students to articulate their ideas and display their skills so that the faculty could perform an accurate evaluation. When we first started teaching this course, no matter what was asked for, people assumed that the only way they could convey the meaning of their experience was to begin on "day one" and describe everything that had happened on every job. This approach overwhelms the student writer, while the product does not satisfy the faculty evaluator. To cut through this process, I tried beginning the course by asking students to articulate a theory; but academic language, presented too early and in the abstract, only intimidates. I tried simplifying the language, asking students to identify what was significant about their work. One said, "The budget. I'm responsible for $500,000." End of remarks. I asked another to tell me what she had learned from her ten years of experience working with the deaf. She, and many who followed her, said she'd "really learned a lot about people." There had to be a better way.

We realized at this point that one of the biggest difficulties students face in the course is a problem of selection. We had to help them choose single incidents that could represent many. We had to help them decide not only what to write but what kind of writing to do. UWW faculty whose training had been in literature and the social sciences carved out the initial design for what we now call a case study. Building on their ideas, we began to ask students to select an incident from work experience that could be conceived of as a problem-solving situation. The task of the student writer was to identify the problem, describe the strategy used to solve the problem, and generalize from the results. Over the years we have clarified the purpose and format of the case study and added supplementary elements to the course. Each refinement represents an effort to help students articulate more fully the link between theory and practice.

This switch to a problem-solving format followed from an important assumption—that thinking and acting not only accompany but affect one another. People who work on the same task do it the same way until it occurs to them that they could do it better or more easily if they changed some part or other of their procedure. Like a scientist testing a hypothesis, a teacher tries a new curriculum, a manager tries a new staffing plan, a counselor opens a therapeutic session in a slightly new way. These are not random moves. Even if they are largely exploratory, each experiment is conducted in light of the practitioner's understanding of a larger goal. In turn, the goal is tempered, modulated, or drastically changed in response to repeated experience and the way that experience is understood. If work didn't make people think, I tell my students, then they would do their jobs on the thousandth day of employment the same way they did them on the first. The challenge they face as student writers is to bring this largely unconscious and perhaps nonverbal thought process to a point where it can be described on paper.

This assumption remains at the heart of the course, though putting it into practice wasn't always easy. When we first started using the case study approach, we assigned it as the first paper for the semester and described it as an exercise in storytelling. Students were asked to write about an incident they considered significant, even if at this point they couldn't say what the significance was. The problem with this approach was identified by the more academically oriented students. They could think of many significant occurrences, but which should they choose, and on what basis? For these students we explained again that each of them has ideas, operating principles, on how work should be done. A counselor of adolescents, for instance, might say that gaining her client's trust by communicating acceptance of his dress, speech, and attitude is an essential first step in establishing a counseling relationship. We explained that the operating principles we were looking for in this course were those students had learned the hard way, through experience, and which they were applying, again and again, in new experiential situations. The task before them was to decide, for the time being, which operating principles were the most important and to choose to write about an experience that demonstrated these ideas in action.

The first papers received for the case study assignment are often a mixed bag. One of the most common problems occurs when a student chooses to describe incidents that have storytelling value, but little else. I remember a community college counselor describing a student who faked a serious illness to get sympathy from her teachers. One day she was seen folding her wheelchair into the back of a station wagon, then getting in and driving away. This story made for great listening, but it didn't work well as an illustration of the principles of academic counseling because the counselor's involvement with this young woman had been limited: the counselor had made few decisions about what action to take. The value of writing a case study, we tell our students, is in the decisions it allows you to discuss. It must show the student grappling with a typical, significant problem, one in which there are a multiplicity of factors and no easy answers.

Despite the difficulties, however, some amazing successes always result. Recently the local director of a federal housing program analyzed a complex situation. He told the story of how he salvaged a building rehabilitation project that had gone awry. He began his paper by commenting on the importance of comprehensive planning at the outset of such a project, along with careful monitoring by those responsible along each step of the way. He was able to illustrate the importance of those principles by describing the difficulties he encountered working with real estate developers whose financial resources were partly imaginary, the potential domino effect of a failure to rehabilitate a major structure in a borderline neighborhood, the political forces he was able to muster to fight for preservation of the project, and the bargain he struck with federal officials who were ready to pull out the matching funds unless deadlines were strictly met.

When students write about the complexities of work roles in a modern society, they both get their message across to faculty evaluators and learn something about writing. It would have been impossible to follow the action in the above story unless the writer carefully defined the problem, defined his role and that of other principal actors, and described each step taken to unravel this bureaucratic nightmare and bring it to a successful conclusion. It was important for the student to know when to summarize events and when to give blow-by-blow accounts, when to remind readers of who was who, when to use transitions that summarized progress, and how to direct readers toward his conclusions.

The case study, then, not only describes how a problem is solved but also makes a point about the particular profession or field involved. The best case studies are about problems that professionals encounter over and over, requiring careful judgment and the ability to balance various factors. When complicated and subtle situations are analyzed, experiential learning is displayed and writing skills are developed.

Despite the success of the case study format, for some students, writing about specific problem-solving strategies on the job makes no sense unless it is preceded by a discussion of the larger personal context from which the vocational choice has arisen. In other words, some people have to tell their stories. After trying for some time to deflect people from this tendency, I changed to the current format in which the first assignment is to write a kind of introduction. I got the seeds for this idea from Charles Moran, who directs the University Writing Program at UMass. These miniautobiographies identify those interests and concerns that led students into the jobs they now hold. To help students avoid getting bogged down or overwhelmed, I try to keep the description of the assignment light: "Explain your life in five pages!" And I remind them that the introduction is just that, a preamble to our real work during the semester. The results are wide ranging. For many the assignment is a major challenge; for others it whets the appetite. I use the paper to diagnose writing problems and to gauge the level of comfort with our subject—the past—before taking on a more structured format. Finally, for those students who would have given me their life stories no matter what the assignment, I use their enthusiasm to start the semester on a positive note and avoid haggling over the specifics of the assignment before we know each other.

Another advantage to giving the introduction assignment before the case study is that it buys time. With three weeks before the first case study is due, students have a chance to think through their selection problems. They read samples of writing done by students in previous semesters. They study the checklists we have developed that outline the components of each course assignment. And they have a chance to work with their staff advisors and with the faculty who will actually recommend the credits they seek. These conferences are a crucial step in the development of the portfolio.

The guidance provided by both the advisor and the faculty evaluator are characteristic of the UWW/UMass emphasis on collaboration. Over the years we have worked out a way to break the task down according to the goals we hope to meet. The course attends to the quality of the writing and thinking that goes into the portfolio. The advisor looks at the portfolio plan to see if the student is asking for credits in areas that are best for the student. Using the expanded vita, an outline of skills and experiences the student writes in the Degree Development Seminar, the advisor pinpoints those experiences that have thematic links and that seem to have taught the student the most. For instance, a teacher's aide may intend to write about classroom experience, but her advisor may point out that her experience running a family daycare center and working as a community organizer gave her skills in working with adults as well as children. This skill could be demonstrated in a case study that emphasizes the way she draws parents into the educational process.

The faculty evaluators view the portfolio process from a somewhat different angle. Their concern, understandably, is with the discipline that they teach. We encourage them to view the student's learning not in terms of the content of a single course but in terms of their overall expectations for students graduating with a major in their department. In the case described above the faculty evaluator might ask the student to write about teaching strategies that include parents, but also to consider how teachers work with students from different cultures, since an understanding of cultural differences is a goal for education majors. Thus, the choices students make regarding topics to address and experiences to describe are made only after several actors have had their say. Our publications say that the portfolio is written in a course, but it is actually begun in our Degree Development Seminar and in a tutorial that involves the UWW advisor and the faculty who represent the university and a discipline. The task of knitting together all these perspectives keeps the UWW advisor and the student on their toes.

But the thoroughness of this collaborative, developmental approach is worth its cost because of the importance of the portfolio in each student's program. Prior learning credits rarely play the role of elective credit in the UWW degree. Most of the time the credits awarded cover one third to one half of an interdisciplinary, professionally focused area of concentration, which in turn accounts for about one half of each degree program. Determining precisely what and how much the student knows and how much he knows is important, not only for the validity of the award but also because it allows the portfolio evaluation to serve as a diagnostic tool. The faculty members involved are encouraged to recommend course work or independent projects that build on what the student knows and fill in the gaps in the student's learning.

Another important aspect of the process that takes place outside the course is determining the number of credits to be awarded. Based on our collective experience with hundreds of portfolios, we have developed a typography. There are three types of portfolios: fifteen credits or fewer; a middle range of about twenty-two, which is the average award; and larger awards of thirty or more. As we move from one category to the next portfolios reflect a wider range of experience and, in most cases, a longer period of years in the field. But more important, they display a deeper understanding of the issues that practitioners encounter, a higher level of skill, a more sophisticated kind of judgment.

Before writing the first case study for inclusion in the portfolio, then, students work both within and outside the classroom to decide what to write about and to develop a sense of the range into which their credit award might fall. Armed with insights and suggestions from both the advisor and evaluators, students complete the introduction and two case studies. Each paper is read aloud in class for peer review and, in addition, receives written comments from the instructor. When the process of revision begins at midsemester, most students have a clear notion of the overall themes of their semester project as well as the subjects of the case studies.

Even with success in defining a problem and detailing the strategy used to solve it, however, students find it difficult to take the final step in each case study and draw conclusions that express a thoughtful point of view. Because of the difficulty, and the importance, of generalizing from experience in the portfolio, we give one final assignment, the principles paper. Its primary purpose is to provide an opportunity to focus on principles of operation, but it also provides a way to combat the exclusivity of the case study format by encouraging students to allude to more than the two or three experiences covered in the case studies.

In explaining this assignment, we ask students to imagine they are educating their replacements. Their task is to write a training manual that summarizes what a practitioner needs to know and be able to do to survive and flourish on the job. I remind them of our discussion early in the semester of the professional priorities that helped them choose a topic for their first case studies. Now they are to discuss these ideas in further detail. Each segment of the paper begins with an operating principle: "A good practitioner should . . ." The writer argues for each principle in the paragraphs that follow, citing numerous examples from experience that show what works and what doesn't work to solve problems. Faculty evaluators learn more about what the student has done, but, more important, they learn about the student's thinking. Gradually, through trial and error, each writer uncovers the hierarchy of values that governs his or her professional life.

Students leave the course with four revised papers, which become sections of the portfolio: an introduction, two case studies, and a principles paper. They also leave with ideas and convictions they didn't know they had. Ironically, many are now ready to take courses that have nothing to do with their experience, while others are ready to compare their own practice with the theories they have examined in the course. In addition to this personal or professional growth, students gain ground as writers. They have had to choose, as short-story writers do, one story that stands for many and take charge of telling that story well. And they have learned that they cannot make much of an impression on an audience without being organized and clear.

Essays written in this course are stories from the front lines of all sorts of human endeavor: designing robots, writing music, boycotting segregated food stores, helping the sick to become well. For teachers, this is an ideal course for those who like to live vicariously. But in addition to gaining a window on the world, those of us at UWW have rediscovered some important assumptions: work makes you learn, and writing about work makes you learn more. We think that when you recognize and build on the strengths adults bring to college, everyone comes out ahead. Adults, black and white, male and female, fulfill the dream of finishing school, and the university benefits from the diversity and challenge they bring. Our liberal experiment is doing fine.

Distance learning programs pose special problems for portfolio development and the assessment of prior learning. As Robert H. McKenzie of the External Degree Program of the University of Alabama explains, "The distance-learning mode creates a special need for structured assignments and supportive deadlines, so that students do not flounder in what is, in the best of situations, a formidable task." Analytical Thinking from Experience serves as both a portfolio development course and as an exploration of the nature of learning. Through its careful, step-by-step method, the course helps students learning at a distance undertake a "College Orientation" by examining the relationship between their knowledge and more formal academic study.

THE EXTERNAL DEGREE PROGRAM, THE UNIVERSITY OF ALABAMA

Robert H. McKenzie

Assessing the prior learning of students who study at a distance poses special challenges both for the students themselves and for the faculty who work with them as advisors and assessors. The face-to-face contact and group encouragement that often constitute a support system for students developing their portfolios is missing in a distance-learning model; without that support system, special curricular and advisory structures must be put into place. In particular, the distance learning mode creates a special need for structured assignments and supportive deadlines, so that students do not flounder in what is, in the best of situations, a formidable task.

Since its inception in 1975 the External Degree Program at the University of Alabama has awarded credit for prior learning based on faculty evaluation of student portfolios. Since 1986 our vehicle for assisting students with portfolio development has been a three-credit, independent-study contract entitled Analytical Thinking from Experience. Although the contract serves as a portfolio development course, much of the contract focuses on elements of learning theory as those elements apply to a student's degree plan and to the work and organization of an institution of higher education. A prior learning portfolio is a possible, but not a necessary, outcome of the contract.

There are several interrelated purposes to the contract. Because many students are interested in how to convert experiential learning into academic credit, the contract is designed to move a student from the notion of "credit for life experience" to the realization that credit is earned for demonstrated *learning* from experience. To help students develop that realization, the contract requires them to move from describing experience to analyzing the learning contained in the experience. Similarly, because students must apply their experiential learning to a degree plan relating to present and future life needs, the contract also contains a series of exercises in self-awareness and degree planning.

In addition, the contract is designed to foster the academic skills and perspectives necessary for success in college. Since the contract requires five written essays, it helps students polish their writing skills; meanwhile, the analysis of experience for the learning contained within it constitutes a series of exercises in critical thinking skills. Finally, because students must relate their experiential learning to the way in which an academic community organizes and conducts itself, the contract introduces students to the nature of academe.

Thus, whatever the range and depth of their experience, students can use the steps in the contract to improve their understanding of self, subject matter, and schooling at the baccalaureate level. The process is organized into a series of explicit, incremental steps that students must complete in order and in a timely fashion, with regular feedback and encouragement from the instructor.

The text for the contract is a workbook, *Analytical Thinking from Experience: A Workbook on Reflection*, which explains the theoretical bases for the contract as a whole and for each step in it. The workbook also provides examples of the exercises required in the contract and explains how to convert the contract exercises into an actual portfolio, or presentation, as it is known in our program.

The contract begins by giving students an opportunity to think about themselves as experiential learners. The first step in the contract is to take the Kolb Learning Style Inventory and to write an essay of personal reaction to the results. The purposes of this first step are for the student to begin reflecting upon experience and for the instructor to obtain an initial reading of the student's writing abilities.

The second step in the contract helps students reflect on the totality of their past experiences by developing what we call a significant learnings outline. This outline is a topical and chronological display of past experiences and includes preliminary ideas about the learning thus derived and how to demonstrate and document that learning. This step allows the students to display all instances of potential college-equivalent prior learning and to begin deciding what might be useful to a degree plan.

The third step in the contract helps students begin to connect past learning to overall educational needs by developing a preliminary degree plan to meet our program's graduation requirements. The objective is to start a conversation, which continues throughout the contract, about a plan for general education and in-depth study of which both the student and the University of Alabama can be proud. By engaging students in a thoughtful conversation about what they want to accomplish, the contract gives them maximum opportunity to exercise adult responsibility in developing a program of study. This step of proposing—and defending if necessary—choices of learning experiences is one of our most important opportunities to help each student establish personal ownership of his or her education. This sense of ownership is an important aspect of the motivation necessary to complete a distance learning program.

The fourth step in the contract asks students to identify the subject area for the prior learning presentation by drafting an application to submit evidence of prior learning. This application records administrative information and designates both the subject area of the proposed prior learning presentation and the area of the student's degree plan to which credit would be applied. The form has four attachments, each of which foreshadows a later step in the contract. This incremental approach to successively more sophisticated mental processes helps students convert the wholeness of the lives they have lived into academic presentations suited to our evaluation process. One attachment calls for a brief description of the experience to be presented. The second calls for a brief description of problems encountered in the experience. The third calls for a brief description of learning from the experience. The fourth calls for a list of possible University of Alabama courses that might be applicable to the student's learning.

Our evaluation process does not operate on a strict course equivalency basis, but it does use existing courses as guides to help students organize presentations. When a student submits a presentation, our staff determines faculty areas required for evaluation and secures permission from each faculty area's dean to use appropriate faculty members. We instruct the faculty member that describing credit recommended in terms of course equivalents is helpful in checking possible credit duplications but that he or she need not be bound by such equivalents as they exist at the University of Alabama. We respect the faculty member's professional capacity to judge the presentation against an overall area of competencies, not just against the way those competencies are organized at this university. If necessary, faculty members from several disciplines evaluate a presentation to ensure that all possible interdisciplinary ramifications are covered.

The fifth step of the contract asks students to describe the *who*, *what*, *when*, and *where* of the experience under analysis in an essay of five hundred words or more. In terms of learning theory, the student describes the concrete experience upon which learning was based. We ask the student to place the experience in a life context, but without writing a life history.

This step involves simple descriptive ability. Most students can accomplish it effectively, but may need some help in ensuring that all significant information is included. This step helps students firmly fix the details of the experience and win the confidence of the reader, who should be fully comfortable with basic facts of the experience before moving to the more difficult analytical parts of a presentation. Here and elsewhere, the contract emphasizes effective written expression.

The sixth step of the contract is a key to moving from description to analysis. It requires students to describe problems encountered in the experience under analysis. This approach is based on what we know about dominant learning styles in our program.

Of the 309 students for whom I have Kolb Learning Style Inventories, 57 percent are oriented toward action rather than reflection as a preferred learning style. Another 25 percent have a higher propensity to grasp reality from experience than from abstract conceptualization. Only 17 percent have an affinity for moving directly from concrete experience to abstract conceptualization. In terms of learning theory, therefore, the sixth step requires students to move from concrete experience to active experimentation rather than directly to abstract conceptualization.

This orientation toward problems encountered is most applicable to those students using the contract to analyze experiences in administrative sciences. We insist, however, that students try this problem orientation no matter what subject they analyze. Students have profitably used this exercise in such diverse subjects as musical performance, photography, religion, textile design, and waste water treatment.

The problem orientation serves as a useful bridge between describing learning experiences and analyzing learning outcomes, the two major essay portions of the presentation format we ask our students to follow. The problem orientation requires that students indicate *how* they have used what they know. A *how* question involves aspects of both description (who, what, when, and where) and analysis (why and what difference it makes). By articulating how they used their knowledge, students begin to analyze experience for the learning it contained.

The seventh step of the contract moves students from the limits of their own experiential learning to the world of expert opinion and the academic organization of knowledge. This objective is accomplished by having students prepare annotated bibliographies of sources they have used in learning about the field. Among others, a benefit of this exposure is that it highlights the comparative dimension important to college-level learning. With exposure to expert analysis of the subject, students have an opportunity to compare their encounters with problems in the field with what experts say about those and similar problems.

In some cases students are already quite knowledgeable about expert opinion in the fields they are analyzing. In many cases, however, student knowledge is confined to a narrow spectrum of opinion on the subject, much of which may be from popular sources. To place their learning in an expert context, students visit a college book store to examine textbooks in the course equivalents they consider applicable. Sources for this step are not limited to written ones. Students often list people as sources of information, sometimes films and radio or television shows. We emphasize an examination of textbooks as a device for better understanding an academic field of study, not as a limit upon resourcefulness.

The world of disciplinary courses is, of course, an artificial world, one that we do not follow slavishly in our program. Still, viewing learning in the context of course equivalents gives form to a degree program and provides parameters of organization and criteria for fairness and lack of redundancy. Moreover, many students find a course structure an initial comfort in the difficult task of accepting responsibility for shaping their own education. Like the examination of text books, the identification of course equivalents helps situate the students' learning in academic organizations of knowledge. This is an appropriate step for students engaged in prior learning assessment, since one aspect of the learning represented in a prior learning presentation is knowledge of how a subject area is organized and delivered in an academic setting.

A related aspect of this evaluation is how a person's learning compares with the way courses are most often organized in progressive steps within a discipline. In many cases a student's learning from experience has occurred at an advanced, specialized level in the context of normal curricular arrangement. For example, a student working in a counseling environment in a job that is equivalent to an advanced-level internship may not have the learning equivalent of a basic introduction to psychology course or of intermediate divisions of the field, such as adolescent, abnormal, or applied psychology. In such a case, older adult students must reflect on the particular shape of their knowledge and judge whether or not obtaining foundation course equivalents makes sense for them.

The eighth step in the contract moves to the key process of abstract conceptualization. This step requires students to draw from their experiences the guiding principles, models, or theories worth passing onto someone else. For many students, this step is difficult, sometimes even intimidating, but it helps students finalize the passage from "experience" to "learning" and situates them as individuals within the community of expertise.

The ninth step of the contract is rather simple and is in accord with what many students presume a presentation of prior learning to be. It requires students to prepare an annotated list of possible documentation for a presentation. We emphasize that documentation supports, *but does not substitute for,* the three key components of a presentation: a narrative essay describing the experience, an analytical essay pinpointing the learning outcomes, and an annotated bibliography putting the first two elements in a conceptual context.

The tenth step of the contract brings the first nine steps into focus. Students reflect on the preceding steps, write an essay discussing any changes that have occurred in self-perception or educational goals, and submit an updated degree plan. Some students find that the contract exercises have clarified their original objectives. Others have made major changes in plans for general or in-depth education. Still other students report feelings of increased efficacy in being able to organize a major project and to write about their past learning effectively.

The eleventh step helps students again look forward after so much concentration on past learning experiences. Students propose a contract for a new learning experience. A student may use this step to develop a proposal to fill in gaps in learning in the area of experience being analyzed in the contract process, to explore a new area if no gaps have been identified, or to develop an initial proposal for a senior project. A students is not required to enroll in the proposed contract, but he or she is encouraged to do so.

Most adult students bring a great deal of experience to their educational undertakings, but, as many researchers have observed, they may have only a weak conceptual grasp of their experiences. They may also bring little understanding of the nature of the academic community and of the meaning of a degree. Analytical Thinking from Experience attempts to address both of these needs. Success in an academic community entails competence in two major skills—the intellectual capacity to think critically and the emotional capacity to persevere in applying that thinking. Our course reflects the belief that adult learning includes the responsibility that should be associated with "adult" as well as the growth that should be associated with "learning."

Competency-based education has one of its most thorough and committed proponents in Alverno College of Milwaukee, Wisconsin. In addition to passing each course as they would in a traditional college, Alverno's students move through a series of developmental levels that mark their growing abilities in various academic competencies. Prior learning assessment grows out of interaction with academic material in the liberal arts and sciences in which new students demonstrate their level of current ability.

Integrated Learning: Strategies and Approaches thus melds the "College Orientation" and "Academic Skills" approaches by actively connecting content and skill. As authors Deutsch, Kramp, and Roth explain, "Assessment shifts the educational emphasis from knowledge as an object or a product to knowledge as an active process of making or doing something with what one has learned, and from the teacher as a repository of knowledge to the student as the agent of learning."

ALVERNO COLLEGE

Bernardin Deutsch, Mary Kay Kramp, and James L. Roth

The curriculum of Alverno College offers women of all ages a liberal arts education, with majors in the traditional arts and sciences as well as in the professional areas of management, education, nursing, and communications. In subject matter, the various courses of study are similar to those of other liberal arts colleges. For the past seventeen years, however, the Alverno faculty has worked to transform the liberal arts curriculum through a dual focus on student ability as well as knowledge.[1] Instead of assuming that abilities develop naturally as a by-product of mastery of subject matter, we explicitly teach students to develop abilities that facilitate the "doing" of what they know.

---

[1]*For a discussion of the evolution of the Alverno curriculum, see* Liberal Learning at Alverno College, *rev. ed. (Milwaukee, 1985).*

The Alverno faculty has identified eight broad areas of ability that it believes characterize the liberally educated adult: communication, analysis, problem solving, valuing, social interaction, responsibility for the global environment, effective citizenship, and aesthetic responsiveness. From our experience of observing effective student performance we have specified six developmental levels for each ability and described each level in behavioral terms so that they can be taught and measured in courses across the curriculum. The descriptive criteria for each ability constitute what we call "ability frameworks," which assist students in mastering the abilities at progressive levels of complexity as they move through the curriculum.

In addition to successful completion of all general education courses required by the college, students must demonstrate, through course-based and comprehensive assessments, the first four levels of all eight abilities. Then, in their major and minor programs of study, they must demonstrate the advanced levels of those abilities that their departments have determined to be central to advanced-level work in those disciplines.

Each course in the curriculum is responsible for providing assessment opportunities for selected levels of selected abilities. The abilities and levels are chosen by the faculty of each department for their appropriateness to the discipline and to the level of the course. The distribution of assessment opportunities among all courses is arranged in such a way that by the time a student has completed all course requirements for the degree, she will also have had multiple opportunities to demonstrate all of the abilities. And since each course beyond the introductory level carries ability prerequisites as well as content prerequisites, the student is assured of encountering those assessment opportunities at developmentally appropriate places in her program of study.

The educational philosophy underlying the Alverno curriculum includes four major assumptions. The first of these is that effective education requires active participation on the part of the learner. Education goes beyond mastery of knowledge to the application of that knowledge, not only for students in advanced level seminars and independent studies but for all students at all stages of the curriculum. Closely related to active participation is the belief that student learning is made most visible through performance. As a result, we have made assessment, that is, the evaluation of student performance according to explicit criteria, a regular part of classroom instruction. Third, we believe that learning increases when students have a clear sense of what they are setting out to learn and what standards they must meet. Finally, we believe it is essential to teach students how to transfer abilities to new situations. Our challenge as a faculty is to help students create frameworks to organize what they already know and apply those frameworks independently. This reflection on both formal and informal educational experiences is what transforms experience into learning.

New students of traditional college age who enter directly from high school are introduced to the principles and assumptions of the Alverno curriculum through the introductory courses in a wide variety of disciplines. In all introductory courses in the natural sciences, social sciences, and arts and humanities, for example, we explicitly teach students to be aware of the ability frameworks and the way students use them to organize their interpretation and communication of ideas. By the time they reach their intermediate and advanced level courses, the habit of searching out underlying constructs and assumptions is a regular part of their approach to learning.

But what happens when nearly half of our entering classes consists not of new students but of older students new to Alverno? Most transfer students and graduates of technical programs at community colleges and hospital schools of nursing have already completed some or all introductory courses by the time they arrive at Alverno. Other returning adult students, those who interrupted their studies years earlier in favor of marriage, family, or work, may have less formal education but a rich set of life and work experiences that, if focused, might constitute the equivalent of introductory college work. All of these students may have the knowledge required to place out of introductory course work, but all may not possess the particular abilities integral to the Alverno curriculum or, if they do possess them, be aware of these abilities.

Given our emphasis on active performance in the present and on the application of prior learning to new situations, both students with college credit and students with experiential learning must demonstrate what they have previously learned to be placed appropriately in their curricular sequences. To assist them in this demonstration, we have designed a transition course, Integrated Learning: Strategies and Approaches, which introduces them to the basic principles of the Alverno curriculum and enables them to draw on their prior learning experiences in a focused way. It also serves as the vehicle for the assessments that determine their placement. The course permits returning and transfer students to situate themselves comfortably within the curriculum after one semester.

Integrated Learning is essentially an immersion in the principles of the Alverno curriculum. The course, divided into sections of about thirty students each, meets six hours per week and carries six semester hours of credit. Students quickly learn that active participation is central to a performance-based curriculum, as they complete three or four assignments each week. These may be analytical worksheets based on their readings, brief two- or three-page papers in which they take and defend positions on issues, write speeches, or prepare for small group simulations. The variety of assignments enables instructors to recognize the strength of different students' learning styles and encourages students to develop a wider repertoire of learning strategies.

The course is organized around the introduction of the eight ability frameworks that define the Alverno degree. Each framework is articulated in terms of behavioral criteria at six developing levels of complexity. Student demonstration of ability at the first four levels constitutes the general education requirement of the college. These are generic criteria in the sense that they are not tied to specific assignments or disciplines and can be translated into the terminology of any discipline. For example, the criteria for analytical ability begin with standards for careful observation (level one). They move on to the ability to distinguish between observation and inference (level two), to posit and explain relationships among observations and inferences (level three), and, finally, to identify and explain organizing principles that account for the structure of an object of analysis (level four). Taken together, these progressive criteria constitute an ability framework for analytical thinking that can be adapted and applied to course work in any discipline.

A similar framework for effective communication emphasizes the process of clarifying and communicating ideas with sensitivity to audience. The valuing framework emphasizes the correlation between belief and behavior as a model for inferring and analyzing values. In the area of aesthetic responsiveness, the criteria form a model for understanding the way formalist analysis, sensitivity to one's own affect, and contextual interpretation are joined to create sophisticated aesthetic judgments. By the end of the semester, returning adult students work with frameworks in all eight areas, something that our traditional-age students accomplish through a variety of disciplinary courses during their first two semesters.

Instructors frequently introduce the eight ability frameworks in relation to students' prior learning and life experience. Problem solving, for example, is a concept familiar to our returning students, but few are really aware of the process they use. Through the exploration of a personal problem solving situation, such as, ''What to do when my supervisor at work asks me to work during time previously set aside to attend class,'' we teach them the general principles of problem identification and problem-solving design. We then introduce problems from the public arena and from disciplines such as environmental science and political science and ask them to apply the same formal problem solving principles to these larger issues.

The cross-disciplinary content of Integrated Learning reflects the fields of study familiar to most students—the humanities, arts, social science and natural science fields. We use one of a number of comprehensive readers that emphasize the methods and epistemological perspectives of the various disciplines. The assignment of a wide variety of shorter, process-oriented readings provides the opportunity to discuss the organizing principles underlying students' prior course work in those disciplines. Our purpose is not so much to provide students with large doses of new information in these fields, something that would be impossible in a single course, as it is to get them to recognize that their prior educational experiences play a major role in their ongoing learning.

As soon as students have worked with an ability framework in class, they are asked to demonstrate that ability in their assignments. The eight analytical reading and listening exercises that students complete throughout the semester are examples of this kind of ongoing formative assessment of student ability. Typical stimuli might include a taped lecture on the cultural importance of art by Suzanne K. Langer or an excerpt from a book on primate behavior by Jane Goodall. In response to each of these articles and tapes of lectures, students complete a detailed worksheet in which they identify the thesis and authorial assumptions and analyze the structure of the communication. After completing the worksheet, but before receiving the instructor's written evaluation, students fill out written self-assessments of the specific strengths and weaknesses of their efforts with reference to the published criteria for effective analytical reading and listening. Finally, the instructors provide written evaluations of both the worksheets and the self-assessments.

These exercises, and similar ones for each of the ability frameworks, are not merely preparation for the prior learning assessment that takes place in the course. They are indeed a part of that assessment. First, they meet our definition of assessment as an observed example of student behavior, performed with conscious reference to explicit criteria, and evaluated by classroom instructors or other expert assessors in terms of those same criteria.[2] Second, to the extent that prior learning contributes to students' capacity to work with all of these ability frameworks in one intensive course, they are opportunities to engage with prior learning using the principles of the Alverno curriculum. As the following example will show, however, the course also includes more formal assessments that both explicitly link prior learning to academic outcomes and call for students to integrate several abilities.

The assessment of prior learning in the arts and humanities is perhaps the most comprehensive in the course. It calls for integration of analysis, valuing, and aesthetic responsiveness, three of the principal abilities taught in all our general education courses in English, history, philosophy, religious studies, and the fine arts. The stimuli for the assessment are pairs of poems, paintings, and excerpts from musical works. In one recent version of the assessment, they included "To Lucasta, On Going to the Wars" by Richard Lovelace and "Dulce et Decorum Est" by Wilfred Owen, "The Third of May" by Goya and "Guernica" by Picasso, and passions by Bach and Penderecki. Students choose to work with one of the three media, based on the level of their experiential backgrounds. Typically, their knowledge will have come from formal course work or perhaps from an avocational interest in writing, painting, or musical performance.

In the take-home assessment, students respond in essay format to as many as eight broad questions of increasing complexity that parallel the developmental levels of these three abilities. Students with relatively little prior learning in the arts and humanities are directed to complete only the first two or four questions, while those with more substantial preparation address six or all eight. The questions begin by asking for explanation of specific ways that the artists' use of form conveys meaning to the student and for explanation of factors in the students' own backgrounds (attitudes, values, life experiences) that condition her unique responses to the works. The questions proceed to elicit more complex comparisons of artistic styles and then to aspects of contextual interpretation. Here, our major concern is that the assessment be fair to students with a wide variety of prior learning experiences. Obviously, a student who has never studied the Napoleonic era or the aesthetic issues of neoclassicism and romanticism will not be able to place the Goya painting in its specific historical context. But she may well have experienced the effects of other wars of have

---

[2]*For a detailed explanation of Alverno's assessment methods, see* Assessment at Alverno College, *rev. ed. (Milwaukee, 1985).*

developed a reflective position on war and violence and will thus be able to respond to the painting in that context. We are interested in her ability to make contextual connections, not whether her prior learning has included the specific content of our courses. The final questions ask the student to make judgments of quality based on a personal aesthetic that expresses her humanistic values.

This assessment as a whole requires a rather complex integration of abilities. We believe this is appropriate since it offers transfer equivalencies up to and including all required general education courses in the arts and humanities. Some students, however, may not be ready to demonstrate their developing abilities in such an integrated format; they tend to be more effective in assessments focused on discrete abilities. We therefore rely on both formative and summative assessments to provide evidence of prior learning.

The evaluation of prior learning and the students' placement in their curriculum sequences rest in the hands of the Integrated Learning course instructors. The students have already received semester-hour credit for previous course work from transfer evaluators in the college's admissions office. What remains at issue is the determination of their levels of demonstrated ability, since all intermediate and advanced courses carry ability prerequisites as well as course prerequisites. If, for example, a student intending to major in psychology has transferred credit for general psychology and human development courses, she will also have to demonstrate in the Integrated Learning course the prerequisite analytical and problem solving abilities for the next course in the sequence, abnormal psychology. If unsuccessful in this effort, she is not required to repeat the two introductory psychology courses, but she does have to take other general education courses that present opportunities to learn and must demonstrate those abilities before continuing her course of study in her major.

At the end of Integrated Learning, the course instructors review student performance on all formative and summative assessments and make an expert judgment of the levels demonstrated by students in all eight areas of ability. They base their decisions on the collegewide criteria for effective performance at each ability and level. Since these public criteria were generated and refined by the faculty as a whole, the course instructors' judgments are essentially a corporate faculty decision. The certification of demonstrated abilities is then recorded by the registrar on student transcripts, and these transcripts are used by the students' academic advisors to place them in appropriate courses.

In the context of the Alverno curriculum, however, assessment does not end with prior learning. We have found that ongoing assessment of developing abilities, both formative and summative, offers definite advantages over more traditional forms of testing and grading. Obviously, the faculty at every college and university require that students read and listen with analytical comprehension. Almost any form of testing that assesses a student product and most recognition exercises will reveal the presence or absence of these abilities. But testing alone, particularly when concentrated near the end of a semester, is primarily an evaluation or control procedure. It reveals degrees of student success or failure, but offers relatively few opportunities for teacher intervention to overcome learning difficulties. The additional components of published criteria, self-evaluation, and feedback help to create a dialog between teacher and student that can lead to improved performance and eventual success by the student. A second advantage of assessment as a learning strategy is the continual exposure to the criteria for effective performance, which helps students to discover explicit ways they can be successful in their work.

There is, of course, the risk that the success they experience in applying the criteria will lead some students to see them as rigid formulas that, if properly applied, will invariably lead to universally valid conclusions. We certainly do not want to leave students with this impression, but there are advantages, from a developmental perspective, in first promoting the criteria as consistent strategies for success. One thing that many of our returning adult students lack is a sense of themselves as independent learners, and the criteria work effectively to generate confidence. At the same time we try to balance this sense of consistency and confidence with exercises that sensitize them to ambiguity and contextual relativism and help them realize that the results of intellectual inquiry may vary according to the approach taken.

One such exercise is the formal assessment for the ability framework for valuing ability, which students complete near the midpoint of the semester. The stimulus is Shirley Jackson's short story, "The Lottery." Students first engage with the story as a homework assignment. In responding to a series of open-ended questions, they use our valuing framework to infer the values represented in the characters, the value conflict that drives the plot, and possibly the value perspective of the author. Up to this point, they have applied the terminology and other conceptual tools learned in class to arrive systematically at the "answers." When they return to class, they meet in small groups and are charged with the task of choosing one character for which they will create new dialog or new situations to alter the character and, concomitantly, the value content of the story. Suddenly, as they experience first-hand the reality of multiple perspectives, there is no single right answer. They have to deal with one another's different valuing orientations. Finally, in the next class, they encounter the story in cinematic form and must come to terms with the existence of two versions of the same story that are quite different in emphasis and style. While the students complete worksheets for the first and third parts of the assessment, the most significant evidence of their learning comes from the self-assessments, where they reflect on the personal impact of this encounter with the complexity of making and interpreting human meaning.

It would be difficult to overestimate the importance of self-assessment as the key to effective learning in the course. For virtually every assignment and assessment, students are asked to specify, with evidence from their work, the ways in which they have met the established criteria. These self-assessments are not the equivalent of students assigning their own grades. Rather, they combine with the instructor's feedback to create a dialog that clarifies the criteria as a set of standards to which both instructor and student are accountable. The self-assessment requirement enables students, again and again, to study the ability frameworks and to see them as learning tools. By continually making specific connections between the criteria and their own performance, they begin to see the behavioral criteria as attributes of the self and not merely as external standards to which they must adhere. For example, "draws relationships between analogous moral issues" becomes a habitual response rather than a requirement. Gradually, they transfer the locus of authority from the instructors to the criteria and finally to themselves as independent learners.

Prior to entering Alverno, very few students have engaged in this particular kind of self-reflection in a systematic way. An obvious reason is that they have never had publicly stated criteria with which to compare their own performances. They have had only limited success in solving the mystery of "what the teacher wants." Another factor limiting public reflection may have been the risk of self-disclosure. In Integrated Learning and throughout our curriculum, we take specific steps to mitigate that risk and promote the reflection essential for productive learning. First of all, ours is a nongraded curriculum. Student achievement is criterion-referenced rather than norm-referenced. Students quickly come to realize that they are competing against a standard and against their own previous performances rather than against their classmates. Since they are not playing a zero-sum game, they have little fear that self-revelation will work to others' advantage and not their own. In fact, self-assessment benefits everyone. It gives other students opportunities to reflect further on their own analogous strengths and weaknesses, and it creates a peer review forum that supplements the feedback of the instructor.

The classroom environment, both for Integrated Learning and for the other courses in the curriculum, reinforces the collaborative, non-competitive emphasis of our system for recording academic progress. Physically, the rooms are decentralized. Instead of always facing the instructor at the front of the room, students sit around tables. Structured small-group activities form a part of the learning strategies for nearly every class session. Here students can try out ideas in a supportive peer group before sharing them with the instructor or the class as a whole. Our roles as instructors are also decentralized. We use the metaphors of coaching and mentoring more often than the traditional one of "professing" to describe our functions. Although they are of our own design, we are as bound by the established criteria for effective performance as our students. Under these conditions, we have found that students are more than willing to engage actively in the discourse of learning and to begin to take responsibility for their own learning.

After successfully completing Integrated Learning and the ability-based assessments associated with the course, transfer students enter the prescribed courses of study for our various majors. Those whose prior education encompassed the full range of general education courses are usually able to move directly to the advanced-level courses and ability requirements of the majors. Others, with less extensive backgrounds, are placed in those courses that enable them to complete the breadth of study we require in the liberal arts and to demonstrate the remainder of the eight abilities at the first four levels. Even those students who do not succeed in demonstrating all the levels of ability that might be expected for a given set of prior educational experiences understand why this is so and what abilities and knowledge they need to develop. Through their work in self-assessment they evolve a better idea of who they are as learners.

Although we have dealt here with assessment as a means for faculty to evaluate adult students' prior learning, performance-based assessment is an active learning strategy used in every course in the curriculum. Assessment shifts the educational emphasis from knowledge as an object or a product to knowledge as an active process of making or doing something with what one has learned, and from the teacher as a repository of knowledge to the student as the agent of learning. Not only does it allow the faculty to measure student knowledge in action, but it also helps the student to take responsibility for her own learning by making her aware of what she contributes to the learning process. By providing explicit standards for effective performance and a classroom structure that facilitates reflection and self-assessment, performance assessment gives the student the means to recognize, name, and organize her abilities, thus enabling her to take advantage of experience and transform it into active learning.

Introduction to Individualized Education, as described by Jane Shipton and Elizabeth Steltenpohl, is one of a number of models developed by Empire State College of the State University of New York and presented in this volume. Students in this study examine "The Meaning of Education" and are introduced to the philosophical debates current in the field of higher education. "Debates over the role of specialization versus general education, of career versus liberal education, and of intellectual versus affective competencies," say the authors, "have constituted aspects of this debate and provide rich material for student reflection and discussion."

EMPIRE STATE COLLEGE, STATE UNIVERSITY OF NEW YORK (A)

Jane Shipton and Elizabeth Steltenpohl

College entry signals transition in adult lives. Adults must make the transition from citizen in the world to student when they enter college. New adult students may lack confidence in their ability to study and learn. They may be uncertain about expectations for college-level work. They may not understand the aims and purposes of liberal arts education. They may lack information about the structure of colleges and universities and the organization of knowledge into disciplines. Their academic skills may be rusty or inadequate. They are strangers in this new world. They may feel they do not belong. They often feel marginal.

Eight years experience as faculty members in the first major college designed specifically for adults convinced us that adults returning to college or entering for the first time would benefit from an introductory learning experience to help them grapple with these feelings of inadequacy and marginality upon entry to college. We felt this experience should provide an opportunity for a realistic self-appraisal of their potential as students, the achievement of a sense of belonging in academe and a deeper understanding of higher education in general and the meaning of a liberal arts education in particular. Further, we believed such an experience would be especially useful before they developed their claim to college credit for prior experiential learning. For the past seven years, we have provided an introductory learning experience using this approach. To date over four hundred adult students have voluntarily enrolled in our four-credit course.

The major goal of our entry course is to empower anxious adults by providing knowledge about self and the institution they have entered so they can become successful participants in a college environment. The course integrates diagnosis and skill building with rigorous content reflecting current thinking about adult development and adult learning as well as the world of higher education. This exploration of the role of education in adult lives gives our students an information base in which to root the identification and description of prior life learning and the degree program planning process.

An immediate aim of the course is to help raise the comfort level of adult students returning to college by providing a group setting. Adults, in our experience, enroll or reenroll in college largely to correct a felt deficiency that is accompanied by a strong sense of urgency. "Here I am," they say, "already forty-two and I haven't got much time left. Everyone else has a degree. I want mine as quickly as possible." Such a student feels unique, the onlyadult in the world who feels so inadequate and under so much pressure to overcome inadequacies quickly. This observation led us to the conviction that these adults need an opportunity to share their anxiety and sense of urgency with others experiencing the same syndrome.

The second focus of the course in building students' confidence is to tap their strength as concrete learners. According to the results of David Kolb's Learning Style Inventory, 71 percent of course participants favor concrete learning modes over abstract conceptual modes. Beginning assignments and activities for the group are devised to draw on the students' strength as concrete learners, while seeking to develop capacities for more abstract thinking and attention to theoretical questions and problems.

In effect, we try to make the group a laboratory for learning how to learn. Throughout the course students complete a variety of readings, exercises, and other assignments, and the outcomes are shared in a nonthreatening atmosphere. This approach has benefits. It enables students to compare their efforts with the reality of their peers' efforts instead of measuring themselves against some imaginary criteria for college work.

Experience convinced us that telling students about their strengths and limitations or what they needed to learn was not useful. We heartily concur with Malcolm Knowles, who says, "If one thing stands out about adult learning, it is that a self-diagnosed need for learning produces a much greater motivation to learn than an externally diagnosed need."[1] Thus, weaving self-assessment of academic skills into the fabric of the study proves to be a most useful device to build the confidence of the well prepared student and to help the student with deficiencies set goals for remediation in a convincing fashion.

We use a variety of self-administering, self-interpreting instruments to help students in their self-diagnosis, for example, the Clarke Reading Self-Assessment Survey (SAS) by John H. Clarke and Simon Wites and the Learning Style Inventory by David A. Kolb. The commonalities of all the self-assessment activities are student control of materials and student responsibility for interpretation. An important aspect of the self-assessment of academic skills is that the task is approached through several types of activities and that the students receive information from multiple sources. While it is easy to disregard one indication of skill limitation or strength, if there are several, the evidence cannot be ignored.

One example might illustrate the method we have tried to employ. The students are asked to write several paragraphs describing an educated person. They compare their writing with student writing samples analyzed by our English faculty and graded on three levels: excellent, college level, and developmental. Students make a judgment about their writing level based on the samples. Later, students complete the word usage, sentence structure, and writing mechanics sections of the Clarke Reading Self-Assessment Survey and score it. In addition, students receive feedback from their mentors on a number of short written assignments and two major ones, a learning autobiography and a final paper in which they consider their educational goals in light of course activities. This combination of information about writing skills reassures the competent and helps those who need remediation to identify and begin their needed work.

---

[1] *Malcolm Knowles and Associates,* Andragogy in Action *(San Francisco: Jossey Bass, 1984), 284.*

This kind of procedure is repeated in relation to other skills such as reading, studying, and thinking. The component parts are usually some kind of open-ended assessment, a checklist perhaps, followed by the use of a standardized self-scoring, self-interpreting instrument, supplemented by feedback from mentors and other students in small and large group discussions.

The content of the course used for this concrete and experiential self-assessment of academic skills begins with the familiar and personal. Students examine their own lives by creating a life map or a narrative account to compare with what has been learned about the life cycle, its crises and transitions, through reading works on adult development by theorists such as Erik Erikson, Daniel J. Levinson, Roger Gould, and Bernice Neugarten. Students determine whether they are ''on-time'' or ''off-time'' according to these theorists. Recognizing college enrollment as an ''off-time'' event for adults gives the students perspective on their discomfort as they begin college and helps explain the urgency they feel with respect to the completion of their studies. Students continue their exploration by examining the personal dynamics of transitions, crises, and change as posed by Erikson and Gould. They consider their roles as workers, family members, and citizens and their development of these roles.

Study of the life course, its crises and transitions, and the dynamics of change helps widen students' focus beyond occupational concerns and rapid degree completion by placing individual fears and educational purposes in a broader conceptual context. Students learn they are normal, not unique or isolated cases. They also learn they are capable of growth and change.

Acquiring knowledge and appreciation of what it means to be an *adult learner* follows study of development as an adult person in our course. The goal is to empower students to take responsibility for their own learning as they have taken responsibility for other areas of their lives as adults.

This goal is met, in part, through the writing of an autobiography focusing on learning situations and outcomes in the students' lives. This autobiography serves several important purposes. It validates prior learning accomplishments in a convincing way, serves as the basis for identifying prior college-level learning for development in their portfolio of advanced standing, and convinces students they have the potential to learn in the future as they have in the past.

Given an expanded sense of self, many begin to question their unexamined assumption that one returns to college simply to get a degree as quickly as possible, or to acquire new occupational skills and find a better job. More than a few students begin to wonder if narrowly focused, occupationally oriented studies would, in fact, fulfill their developmental needs or satisfy their curiosity as learners. Students extend their consideration of adult development by reading Rita Weathersby's *Life Stages and Learning Interests*. They maintain a daily journal of interests, questions or problems that need solving as posed by newspapers, television, film, the workplace, the community, and the world. They experience the self as normal, multifaceted, and capable of growth.

To initiate the sessions on adult learning, we ask students to assess themselves on the competencies of self-directed learning as identified by Malcolm Knowles. In doing this, most students rate themselves high on being nondependent and self-directed persons, but rate themselves low on their ability to diagnose their learning needs, to translate their needs into objectives, to identify strategies and resources for achieving objectives, and to evaluate outcomes.

To open up this subject for students, readings are undertaken in sources such as *The Adult Learner, A Neglected Species* and *Self-Directed Learning* by Knowles. To test ideas from the readings in a concrete fashion, one assignment asks students to interview another adult student of their acquaintance and to reflect as well on their own experience relating to the characteristics of adult learning, including the role of experience in learning and the process of learning most congenial to adults. Students also consider the differences between self-directed and teacher-directed learning.

Confronting the meaning of what it is to be an adult learner leads to a transition in the students' views of themselves as learners. In addition to diagnosing their own learning needs, they begin to see a place for developing an educational plan and carrying out specific learning activities. They start to take responsibility for their own learning. This is a critical step in becoming a successful college student.

Exploring the meaning of higher education, including its development historically as well as its scope and purposes today, has constituted another significant area of study in our course. Indeed, it is an essential element in achieving an understanding of what it means to be an educated person considered both in terms of competencies and in terms of subject matter. This is important because based on every measure used with the students the large majority take a highly pragmatic or instrumental view of education.

At the start of our consideration of higher education, we ask students to list specific areas of study in which they are interested and those they know nothing about. The typical reply under areas of interest includes topics of occupational study. Mathematics, science, and the humanities are listed as areas of little or no interest or no prior knowledge. In our view, this is a limited background with which to undertake goal setting and program planning in college.

The question of what best comprises a college education is, in fact, a controversial issue in higher education in the United States today. Debates over the role of specialization versus general education, of career versus liberal education, and of intellectual versus affective competencies constitute aspects of this debate and provide rich material for student reflection and discussion. Thus, in this phase of their work, students read and discuss excerpts from reports that have appeared from college campuses, scholarly groups' foundations, and government bodies, each with its own recommendations and rationales for undergraduate education. Examples of these reports are *Higher Learning in the Nation's Service* from the Carnegie Foundation for the Advancement of Teaching, *Integrity in the College Curriculum: A Report to the Academic Community* by the Association of American Colleges, and *Involvement in Learning: Realizing the Potential of American Higher Education* of the U.S. Department of Education. Students also read articles that explore the interrelationship of career and liberal education, such as "Integrating Liberal Education, Work and Human Development" by Arthur Chickering and "A Businessman Looks at the Liberal Arts" by Arthur Oppenheimer.

For more concrete activities students analyze college catalogs, peruse daily newspapers for articles on higher education, sketch timelines on the development of the university, and listening to faculty speakers in various fields. Terms such as *liberal arts, general education, rational thinking, science, classical education, humanities, advanced-level-study,* and *disciplines* and *interdisciplinary study* begin to take on substantial meaning. Our goal is that a knowledge base be formed about the nature of education that can lead students to more thoughtfully address the questions of purpose and content in planning their own college education.

Indeed, in the course's final assignment, a paper describing the impact of this study on their educational goals, students reveal a transition in their understanding of higher education. Many move from a solely career-oriented focus to one that includes specific topics or competencies in general education as well as to an appreciation of the expressive values of education. Some come to see the foundations of liberal learning in their work or civic experiences that can be built upon in various ways in their college study.

Our experience has convinced us that adult students can overcome feelings of marginality or inadequacy in resuming their education. They are helped through these feelings by a supportive group of peers, experiential learning activities, self-assessment opportunities, and a specially planned curriculum that includes study of adult development, the characteristics of adult learning, and the purposes of higher education. These factors then provide a foundation for the successful development of students' descriptions of prior college-level learning and for the creation of individual curricula in their degree programs. Furthermore, the examination of their interests and deficiencies during the transition course prepares them to generate a wide range of topics for further study, both general and focused, liberal and applied. Last and perhaps not least, students' understanding of the stages of adult development and their own place in the life cycle reduces their sense of urgency to complete a degree as quickly as possible.

In her final paper, one forty-five year old student, Beverly, describes her experience in the course this way:

> Through this course, I have been able to assess where my strengths and weaknesses lie, to discover my learning style, to understand how this educational venture fits into the larger picture of my life, and to map out strategies both practical and academic for forging joyously ahead.

As with the Introduction to Individualized Education described by Jane Shipton and Elizabeth Steltenpohl, "The Meaning of Education" forms the focus of the course developed by the External Student Program of Ohio University. In this model, however, it is through the analysis of the student's own experience that the "meaning" of education comes through. As explained by Suzanne Boyd, the program makes explicit what is implicit in all quality prior learning assessment, namely, the importance of the distinction between experience and learning. "In trying to understand the concept of experiential learning," says Boyd, "the student begins to examine experience for changes in behavior, feelings, knowledge, and skills that were by-products of the experience. Thus, the process of separating experience from learning begins."

This essay is also interesting as a second example of quality prior learning assessment conducted through a nonclassroom-based, distance model.

EXETERNAL STUDENT PROGRAM, OHIO UNIVERSITY

Suzanne Boyd

Ohio University is something of an anomaly among institutions known for services for adult students: it is a traditional residential undergraduate school of about fifteen thousand students; it is quite remote from population centers, located as it is in the foothills of the Appalachians in southeastern Ohio; and it is part of the state university system, with no special mandate to serve adult students. Nonetheless, Ohio University offers two programs of interest and service to adult learners: a highly respected program of portfolio development, and an External Student Program (ESP) that allows adults who cannot come to the campus to pursue degrees.

When these two programs were being developed in 1977, it was determined that they should be linked. The reasoning was that ESP students were highly motivated adults who had proved they could work well independently and therefore were exactly the sort of students likely to do well in the portfolio process. What was less certain was the importance of the portfolio class itself. How necessary was the group support, the chance to explore values or career issues, the access to "model" portfolios, or the face-to-face interaction with the instructor? Could materials or services be developed that might make up for the lack of class contact?

To help students compensate for the lack of group support and class contact, a study guide consisting of six lessons and including some samples from actual portfolios was developed in 1981 as the first students were being admitted into the independent study method of portfolio development. In addition, four 30-minute videos were developed under a Kellogg grant to supply some of the missing class contact. Finally, the office was equipped with an 800 number so students could speak with their instructors.

Although the basic format is the same, the study guide has since undergone a number of revisions aimed at clarifying the process for the ESP student, and a second book has been added. It contains sample pieces from a variety of portfolios, plus one more complete portfolio with annotations. The videos were found to be unnecessary and eliminated. Our students' success with the materials suggests that distance assessment can work and that courses can be designed to allow students to develop portfolios outside of classroom-based workshops.

Ohio University's external students come from every state in the Union and from seventeen foreign countries. Certain of these students, roughly 10 percent, are recommended for the portfolio program by an ESP advisor, who assesses the relevance of their experiential background for their degree design and their ability to express themselves in writing. If their writing skills need polishing, a writing course that can be taken by correspondence is recommended. Once they are enrolled in portfolio development and receive the course materials, they have a calendar year to complete the course. They are asked in the first lesson to develop a timetable for completion, which helps them and their instructor to monitor their progress.

The study guide takes them step by step through the process necessary to develop a portfolio at Ohio University. Lesson one, in addition to helping them set completion goals, has some written exercises that encourage them to think about themselves as learners and about previous positive and negative learning experiences. For instance, students are asked to consider such questions as, "Under what conditions are you most effective in life and career pursuits, with imposed external controls or your own internal control? Does this apply to you as a learner, too?'' Students are then asked to submit three short essays: their ''most rewarding'' learning experience, their ''least rewarding'' learning experience, and the image they have of themselves as learners. Students are free to interpret these questions in any way they choose, and they report that they learn much about themselves in the process.

These essays are preliminary explorations and are not included in the final portfolio. They constitute a kind of warm-up for the lessons to follow and allow the instructor to assess both writing ability and analytical skills. Lesson one also discusses experiential learning using David Kolb's four-step model. Lessons two and three take them through the process of developing the goals and the chronology. Each lesson is sent to the instructor for comments and then is returned to the student. In addition, students are encouraged to call in on our toll-free line whenever they have a question.

Lesson four is probably the most critical lesson in the study guide.[1] It consists of a worksheet that asks students to separate their learning from their job title, experience, or duties and then to relate that learning to specific Ohio University courses. Students make their course selections at this point by utilizing two resources: the Ohio University catalog that contains descriptions of all undergraduate courses regularly taught at the university and a special appendix in the back of the study guide that supplies some ''inside'' information about course selection in various departments and lists the more than five hundred courses that have previously been awarded through for credit experiential learning.

Lesson four was created to try to help students separate learning from experience in a columnar format; to the extent that a student does it well, it serves as an outline for the learning statements that are the subject of the next lesson. Students are asked to list experiences, responsibilities, tasks—the stuff of which resumes are made—in

---

[1]Although I have taught Portfolio Development on campus and by independent study for several years, I found it surprisingly difficult to write about the process that students go through in separating experience from learning. This is no doubt because teaching it is one thing, wrestling with the issues by actually doing it another. In one sense, this is what experiential learning is all about. Therefore, I asked an ''expert''— Katharine Terrie, one of my current students—to write about what she was experiencing in trying to separate her learning from her experience. Some of what is included in the discussion of lesson four is hers.

one column and opposite that column to describe what learning was derived from each experience. This exercise is the culmination of the separation process. The student looks at his or her experience and asks the question, "What did I learn or what do I know now that I did not know before assuming these responsibilities?"

After some practice, the separation process becomes easier because the mindset has changed. The student is now focusing on learning, that is, changes in behavior, judgment, feelings, skills, knowledge— not experiences or responsibilities.

The chart created in lesson four is, of course, different for each student. One student, who had been a commercial loan officer and compliance officer, identified the following duties and responsibilities and then translated those activities into the learning and skills that resulted:

Description of Duties and Responsibilities *or Activities*

Initiated, executed, documented, serviced commercial, consumer, and agribusiness loans. Performed collections, collateral evaluations, and liquidations. Prepared Small Business Admin. loans, responded to credit inquiries, performed financial analysis, presented loan requests in written and oral form to executive committee. Served as backup for cashier: sold or borrowed funds to balance bank's liquidity, handled investments for bank and customers. Supervised conversion of loan portfolio to computer. Interpreted federal regulations and implemented them into bank policy.

Learning and Skill *That Resulted*

Learned value of concise communication, written and oral. Learned basic credit principles and policies and effects of these policies within banking system and in the economic community. Learned tax consequences on farm, ranch, wholesale, distributor, retail businesses. Acquired skill in liquidations, bankruptcy proceedings. Learned legal aspects of commercial paper, consumer credit, and secured transactions as covered by the UCC. Learned accounting procedures for corporations: stock transactions, investments, depreciable assets; and partnership and proprietors. Learned relation of money, debt, and economic activity. Became proficient in computer basics and in financial software. Learned role of financial management in business enterprises; performed extensive financial analysis, including budgeting for businesses, working capital use, and planning for short- and long-term funds.

This same student then identified the following courses as equivalent to his experiential learning:

Accounting 202
Managerial Acct (1)

Computer Systems in Business 200
Intro to Business Computing (4)

Finance 325
Managerial Finance (4)

Business Law 357	*Economics 360*	*Finance 450*
Law of Commercial	Money and Banking (4)	Credit and Lending
Transactions (4)		Principles (4)

Management 325J
Business
Communications (4)

This lesson also has a number of significant benefits for the staff members who work with students. First, a copy of this lesson is sent to the external student advisor for a second check to ensure that the courses the student wishes to seek through portfolio are useful to his or her degree. Second, it has been useful as a summary sheet in cases where faculty have had to be consulted about the relevancy of a student's background for a particular course. Finally, it gives the instructor a better idea of the student's background and possible documentation for requesting a certain course. The final selection of courses to be requested is negotiated by the student and the instructor, often in writing, but occasionally by phone. When the instructor has commented on the course selections and perhaps suggested others that the student has not considered, additional information in the form of syllabi, previous evaluations, or special directions is sent to the student. Frequently the student will refine his or her selections after comparing learning with actual course requirements.

The process we ask students to undertake in lesson four is one that many find difficult. My students say that delineating the distinction between experience and learning takes practice. Most students think and speak in terms of experience, without realizing that sometimes they mean experience, sometimes they mean learning, and sometimes they mean both.

One student reports that she was forced to reread and rethink lesson one as she completed lesson four. Lesson one, she points out, first introduces the phrase "experiential learning," that seems to be a combination of experience and learning and in some respects is. In trying to understand the concept of experiential learning, the student begins to examine experience for changes in behavior, feelings, knowledge, and skills which were by-products of the experience. Thus the process of separating experience from learning begins.

Separating learning from experience to accomplish the objectives of Portfolio Development is not done in a vacuum, however. At the same time that students are thinking about distinguishing learning from experience, they are beginning to think about turning learning into course credit. The writing assignments that lead up to developing learning statements in lesson five are all designed to point students in the direction of separating learning from experience and then to force them to take a realistic look at that learning to determine if it can be translated into college credit.

It is during lesson four and the two lessons that follow that most telephone contact with students occurs. Some students require extra encouragement at this time, and some are bewildered by the choices available to them. Some simply need to have their attention redirected to the resources they have at hand but have not assimilated thoroughly, or they need to have the university bureaucracy reinterpreted for them. By this time the instructor has had the benefit of reading the goals paper, the chronological record, and the introspective pieces prepared in the first lesson, and so has some sense of the student as a person. We believe this is an important feature of our portfolio coursefor ESP students: though it is done by independent study, it is not in any way impersonal.

Lesson five deals with writing the learning statements, using the worksheet in lesson four as an outline. The sample portfolio used as the text provides the guide to form; the guide to class content comes from the appendix references in the study guide, course materials sent when lesson four is returned, and, occasionally, contact with a faculty member by letter or phone. The finished learning statements are submitted to the instructor with a list of possible documentation for his or her critique.

Lesson six, the final lesson, details the compiling of the actual master and miniportfolios. Master portfolios, which contain the goals statement, the chronology, and learning statements and documentation for all the courses a student is requesting, are submitted in large ring-binders and are retained in the ESP office. The material in the miniportfolios duplicates that part of the master that pertains to a single course. The miniportfolios are sent for assessment to faculty members who teach the courses themselves. Once the assessment is complete, the miniportfolios are returned to the student.

Our experience with the ESP students has shown that the on-campus class participation is not a factor in completing a portfolio or in receiving requested credit and that ESP students are at least equally likely to complete the process. On the average, ESP students request more courses than on-campus students, perhaps because many ESP portfolio students are driven by career advancement interests and come from experiential backgrounds where they have participated in substantial on-the-job training, seminars and workshops. In addition, we have some ESP students (pilots, for example) whose professional credentialing matches courses of study at the university especially closely, making documentation a relatively easy matter. Like our on-campus students, ESP students receive about 90 percent of the credit they request, provided they are willing to submit extra documentation or submit other kinds of verification, such as test results. Approximately one third of the portfolios returned from faculty request additional information, although our faculty occasionally call students, or their documentation references, on their own.

As the External Student Program has continued to grow, so has the number of ESP students compiling portfolios. In the past year ESP students accounted for about one third of all students admitted to the portfolio program: 56 of 155 students.

In short, our experience has shown that, at least for a course-match system like ours, in-class participation is not critical for success in the portfolio development process, provided a great deal of personal attention and direction and adequate resources are available. We have found this to be true not only for the highly talented and motivated individual who will do well in any process but also for the student who is far more timid and unsure of his or her skills.

What are the key ingredients for the success of this program? We believe there are several: (1) connection to our strong and well-managed External Student Program; (2) careful selection into the program and continued advising and coordination of degree planning; (3) clear study materials to guide the student working independently; (4) easy telephone access to the instructor; and (5) a University that is responsive to the needs of adults in terms of its policies and procedures and that allows a wide range of possible courses for assessment.

Metropolitan State University in St. Paul, Minnesota offers another approach to portfolio development within a competency-based system. Perspectives: Educational Planning and Philosophy explores "The Meaning of Education," including "what it means to be an educated person in today's society, how that relates to other times and other societies, and how educational choice is constrained by gender, race, and class," as author Leah Harvey explains. Simultaneously, through its unique "theory seminars," Metro State helps students gain credit for practical knowledge by augmenting it with theoretical study.

METROPOLITAN STATE UNIVERSITY

Leah Harvey

Metropolitan State University was founded in 1971 as an upper-division university with a mission to serve adult students. Consistent with this mission, Metro State has developed a unique educational approach based on our philosophy of adult education: a belief in flexible, competency-based educational frameworks; student authority over curricular decisions; and life-long learning.

Our use of flexible, competency-based educational frameworks is based on the conviction that graduation requirements fitting everyone into the same pattern often frustrate individual educational goals and are not appropriate for adult students. Thus, instead of listing curricular or distribution requirements, Metro State identifies five areas of competence that provide a framework for students' undergraduate educational programs. These five general areas are communication; community; vocation; culture, science, and tradition; and avocation.

Metro State defines competences as what a student knows and can do in a particular subject; it must include both theoretical and practical knowledge. Consequently, although most Metro State students complete a specified number of courses when working toward their degrees, they may use other learning strategies to achieve competence. Metro State recognizes the university-level learning students gain through prior experience and encourages them to look at alternatives to courses, such as independent studies and internships. All student learning is recorded on a narrative transcript that includes the competences, the way they were attained, and written evaluations of each one.

An important part of Metro State's mission is to help our students develop as lifelong learners, that is, learners who are able to establish their own goals and objectives and achieve those objectives using community resources. This approach, which is built into our degree-planning process, presupposes that students have the ability, the experience, and the desire to make responsible educational choices and assumes that, with appropriate guidance, they will accept that responsibility.

Metro State therefore offers students primary authority over the content and direction of their degree programs and requires that they play responsible roles in planning and implementing their own educational programs. Students design their own individualized degree programs with advice from the faculty, using the broad framework of competences discussed above.

Planning begins in Perspectives: Educational Planning and Philosophy, the one course required of all students. In it, they examine what it means to be an educated person in today's society, how that relates to other times and other societies, and how educational choice is constrained by gender, race, and class. Using this examination of the meaning and function of education as a basis, students design degree plans that include prior learning as well as future classroom and nonclassroom learning.

To provide a context for developing liberal arts degree programs, students are assigned readings about education and about current educational and cultural debates. They may, for example, read excerpts from John Dewey, Jerome Bruner, Paulo Freire, and Alfred North Whitehead on philosophies of education. In addition, they may read discussions of the traditional educational corpus, such as *Cultural Literacy* by E. D. Hirsch and *World of Ideas* by Bill Moyers, as well as readings in the areas of cultural diversity such as *Black Elk Speaks* by John G. Neihardt, *Multi-Cultural Literacy* by Rick Simonson and Scott Walker and *The Souls of Black Folk* by W.E.B. Dubois. The working text for the course, *Individualized Educational Planning*, written by Metro State faculty members, is accompanied by *The Educated Person: A Collection of Contemporary American Essays*, edited by Professor T. Jones. Assignments and class discussions are designed to engage students in the debate about what college education should be and to empower them to participate in planning their own programs.

Using the five competence areas as an educational framework, students identify the learning outcomes they have attained through prior learning and experience, the previous course credits they have in those areas, and the outcomes they plan to attain while at Metro State through courses, internships, structured independent studies, or individualized learning contracts. When completed, students' plans are reviewed and approved by faculty members working in the specific vocational areas as well as by those who review them from the perspective of a liberal arts degree. Full-time faculty members are responsible for final plan approval.

Like all the learning outcomes reflected in a Metro State degree plan, those gained through the assessment of prior learning must be articulated as discrete competences in specific subjects. A competence is equivalent to the amount of learning usually gained in a four-credit, upper-division university course. Learning may be included in a Metro State degree if it has a theoretical basis, is equivalent to university-level learning, and is appropriate to a student's educational goals and a liberal arts degree program.

During the planning course, students identify any prior learning they want to include in their degree programs, pending direct evaluation by appropriate disciplinary experts. In addition to articulating their prior learning, students are required to gather evidence to document the process by which they gained it. Then, for each area of learning, a faculty member with expertise in the field assesses the learning using two or more measurement techniques: written exams, oral interviews, situational observations, product evaluations, or simulations. By using Metro State faculty to evaluate students' previously acquired nonacademic learning, the university is assured that credit is awarded only for academically sound, university level knowledge.

In all of the above procedures, Metro State is similar to other institutions that offer high-quality assessment of prior learning. Over the years, however, it became apparent to the faculty that the assessment process often ignored an important quality of experiential learning. Although students came with extensive practical expertise, this expertise often lacked the theoretical component usually expected at the university level. For example, students coming from a background in business might know management techniques, yet not have a sufficient understanding of the theories of motivation and human behavior that provide the framework for those techniques. To address this problem, a new learning format—a theory seminar—was designed to augment practical learning with more academic knowledge.[1]

Because Metro State courses have always emphasized both theory and practice, students with extensive practical learning were often faced with two unsatisfactory options—taking a course that included the practical learning they already had or completely omitting from their educational programs learning they had gained in the field. With the theory seminars students have a third option, that of adding some new learning to prior experiential learning. Theory seminars are not short courses; they assume, and are designed to build on, extensive previous learning. In this format students with extensive experience and knowledge in a subject meet with similarly experienced students and with faculty in short classroom sessions to supplement their practical learning in a subject with more academic knowledge.

Metro State faculty have developed theory seminars in more than 30 subject areas.

1. Communication Skills
    - Interpersonal Communication
    - Managerial Communication
    - Spanish
    - Writing

2. Professional Expertise
    - Chemical Dependency Counseling
    - Compensation Management
    - Contract Administration Under Collective Bargaining
    - Counseling
    - Criminal Justice
    - Human Services Administration
    - Management
    - Marketing
    - Nursing Leadership and Management
    - Public Relations
    - Supervision
    - Victimization
    - Volunteer Personnel Management

---

[1]*The theory seminar concept was developed by Dean Leah Harvey and Professor Anne Webb with a two-year grant from the Fund for the Improvement of Secondary Education (FIPSE).*

3. Civics
   - Community Leadership
   - Political Effectiveness
   - Volunteerism

4. Art and Culture
   - Literary Analysis
   - Music
   - Sport in American Culture
   - Studio Arts and Crafts
   - Television and Society
   - Travel and Culture

5. Other
   - Computer Algorithms
   - Freshwater Fishing
   - Investments
   - Parenting
   - Religious Studies

The purpose of these theory seminars is to augment prior learning, to integrate practical and theoretical learning, and to use both in looking to the future. This practical and theoretical learning, and the relationship between them, forms the curricular focus in theory seminars in a wide variety of fields.

The particular relationship between theory and practice, however, varies from seminar to seminar, depending on the field under study. In some fields, faculty members see their most important task as filling in the gaps in students' knowledge with factual academic content in the subject. In others, the faculty considers it most important for students to analyze a variety of significant theories and models and learn to apply them to particular situations. Thus, the theory seminar in Marketing concentrates on accumulating factual information on matters such as pricing and distribution, with less emphasis on understanding a variety of theoretical models built from that factual information. On the other end of the continuum, in Parenting, students often have a base of factual knowledge (the age at which children say "no" or solve complex verbal problems, for instance), but need to examine the theories which have been developed to interpret these facts and to guide the behavior of adults toward children.

The content of the theory seminars grows from our understanding of those components important to university-level learning, a subject which the faculty has discussed in many forums. In addition to theory and practice per se, the faculty has identified issues of communication and methodology as integral to most disciplines. Communication skills are covered in many theory seminars, as are such subject-specific forms of critical analysis as scientific inquiry and literary analysis. Similarly, Metro State is committed to considering issues of gender, race, and class in all learning. This emphasis is often not a part of the learning students gain independently and is therefore integral to most theory seminars.

Faculty have identified other areas of learning present in all disciplines, but not necessarily covered in all theory seminars because other areas of knowledge are deemed more important. Included here is a focus on multiplicity and relativity of perspective. Theories of management and theories of child development, for example, are both products of an historical chronology, occurring in part because of the historical culture of their formulators and developing from and incorporating aspects of theories and models that have gone before them. Thus, an historical examination of the rise of theories may form part of a theory seminar. Equally important for a broad perspective is an awareness of assumptions, values, frames of reference, and points of view, including those of both faculty and students.

Finally, all fields include ethical and aesthetic considerations. Theory seminars may therefore examine the professional codes of ethics of such fields as public relations and counseling or such legally imposed ethical codes as affirmative action in management, narcotics legislation in nursing, and constitutional rights in criminal justice. Issues of aesthetics and style, in turn, are not confined to literature and the arts. Theory seminars may examine styles of communication, management, and leadership, many of which hold within them concepts of beauty and aesthetic fulfillment.

Learning is an ongoing process. Thus, theory seminars emphasize not only prior and current knowledge but the way knowledge can be integrated into future learning and growth. We hope that by viewing their prior learning in a larger context students will recognize the potential for using all past and new knowledge as a basis for lifelong learning.

Theory seminars include five components: self-scoring diagnostic tests; preseminar assignments; structured class sessions ranging in total time from eight to fifteen hours; individualized assignments; and an evaluation session.[2] While each seminar is different, the following is a typical format.

---

[2]*This section is a revised excerpt from Anne Webb and Leah Harvey,* Theory Seminar Handbook *(St. Paul, MN: University of Minnesota, 19), 39–45.*

The first step in the theory seminar process, completed before the seminar itself gets under way, is that of diagnostic testing. The purposes of diagnostic testing are, first, to give students the information they need to choose appropriately among a course, theory seminar, or evaluation of prior learning, and, second, to give instructors information to use in planning what needs to be covered in a theory seminar. Diagnostic tests can also be organized so that students can identify and address weaknesses prior to a first theory seminar meeting.

Thus, the tests emphasize the extent and nature of students' practical experiences, a middle range of knowledge or expectations for the field, and the theoretical knowledge one might expect students to have gained through prior experiences. Because diagnostic tests are used for advisory purposes only, the emphasis is on brevity rather than reliability. They are brief and easy for students to take and for instructors to score. Self-scoring tests are the most efficient.

Before the first session of any theory seminar, the faculty member must clearly define his or her expectations of what experiential learning students should bring to the theory seminar and any reading or other advance preparations expected of students. Because of the short amount of actual classroom time and the varied advance preparation of the students, theory seminar syllabi are generally sent out early and students are expected to complete specified work prior to the first session. Assignments completed before the first session prepare students for informed class discussion and analysis and make more efficient use of the first meeting.

Once the seminar itself has begun, the faculty member encourages students to bring their experiential knowledge into the classroom. In the Counseling seminar, for example, students write accounts of methods and resources they have used with clients and prepare detailed written descriptions of their training.

A wide variety of learning strategies heightens the learning potential for all students in the seminar. They include role plays, simulations, case studies, and small group or team assignments. In the Community Leadership seminar, for example, students work in groups on a particular organizational problem assigned by the instructor. Participants have specific roles to play in the organization. In the Chemical Dependency Counseling seminar, students are given a situation from literature, such as Edward Albee's *A Delicate Balance* or Lillian Helman's *The Little Foxes*, and then work in groups to develop a case study using either psychosocial or sociocultural perspectives. Similarly, students in both Human Services Administration and Marketing seminars are asked to work in small groups to research topics and present the results in formal, in-class presentations.

Since students come to the seminars with different backgrounds, it is important to **identify what individual students need to learn to fulfill the learning** parameters of the theory seminars. This is accomplished by clarifying theory seminar objectives and by individualizing seminar assignments to fit each student's needs. These independent assignments generally emphasize analysis and communication and use individualized and group projects and individualized reading assignments to fill in those gaps.

As it is neither possible nor desireable to separate teaching and evaluation, assessment is integrated into the entire theory seminar process. Most theory seminars, however, include a final evaluation session in which students make presentations and, if appropriate, critique each other's work.

The emphasis on identifying prior learning and augmenting that learning through theory seminars has been successful at Metropolitan State University. It gives students the opportunity to use prior learning in their degree programs in a supportive environment. Diagnostic tests are usually self-scoring, so there is little financial or personal risk to students, and students who have successfully completed diagnostic tests can be reasonably sure they have the knowledge needed for successfully finishing those theory seminars. Also, theory seminars give experienced adults the opportunity to learn from one another in a collegial environment.

Faculty, too, benefit from this type of learning. First, they have the opportunity to work with students who have been selected based on their knowledge and experience. In almost all cases faculty find the level of classroom discussion in theory seminars to be higher than that found in more traditional classes. Student projects, integrating theory and practice, offer instructors new insights into current issues in their fields, insights often missing from their more academic work. Further, developing a theory seminar, a new approach to teaching, gives the faculty a unique opportunity for professional development. Those who participate in the process of developing theory seminars find that their approaches to teaching, in general, have become more interesting and innovative.

The Harry Van Arsdale Jr. School of Labor Studies of Empire State College offers a unique curriculum of interdisciplinary social sciences that focuses on the study of work. Educational Planning: An Introduction to Labor Studies merges "The Experience of Work" approach with "Introduction to a Field." According to author Elana Michelson, "the very subject matter of labor studies ... brings the experience of workers into academic focus .... Thus, there is an organic relationship between the self-exploration required of students for purposes of portfolio development and those same students' introduction to the methodology of their major field."

HARRY VAN ARSDALE JR. SCHOOL OF LABOR STUDIES, EMPIRE STATE COLLEGE, STATE UNIVERSITY OF NEW YORK

Elana Michelson

The Harry Van Arsdale, Jr. School of Labor Studies (SLS) was established in 1971 to provide an undergraduate education focusing on the interdisciplinary study of work, workers, and workplace empowerment. Although part of Empire State College, SLS serves a special and unique constituency of trade unionists, working-class community activists, and advocates for such work-related issues as quality healthcare benefits and occupational safety and health. Demographically, SLS students span the greater New York workforce: Black, White, and Hispanic; male and female; public and private sector; apprentices, active and unemployed workers, and retirees.

As a college for workers who wish to study issues concerning work, SLS posits a unique linkage between the prior learning of its students and the academic curriculum. The very subject matter of labor studies—the meaning and role of work in human life, the power relationships that arise within the workplace setting, the technical skills of labor relations, the social and economic environment in which industrial structures and technological change evolve—brings the experience of workers into academic focus. Moreover, the overwhelming part of students' experiential learning arises through work experience, either directly as job skills or indirectly through trade union or other organizational activity. Thus, there is an organic relationship between the self-exploration required of students for purposes of portfolio development and those same students' introduction to the methodology of their major field.

Portfolio development at SLS therefore takes place within a course whose dual title is both intentional and to the point. Educational Planning: An Introduction to Labor Studies allows the past experience of the students as workers to serve a double purpose. As in any prior learning assessment program, portfolio development provides a format for assessment and credit recommendations; at the same time, articulating their past experience and knowledge presents students with a model in miniature for studying the phenomenon of work. In effect, the individual life experience of the students serves as the smallest of a series of concentric circles that expand into a fuller and more complex understanding of the economics and sociology of work as students move through the course and the curriculum.

Educational Planning classes at SLS vary a good deal depending on the particular mix of students and programs and the particular faculty member. All, however, have the same basic strategy: to use students' own experience both to develop a sense of personal attainment and to establish the foundations for further study of the experience of workers as a whole. The following description is thus both generic and idiosyncratic; it traces the curriculum that one faculty member might develop for particular groups of students.[1]

Educational Planning: An Introduction to Labor Studies begins with an examination of the phenomenon of work. Readings on this issue often span the religious and political spectrum: students may read selections from Biblical, Talmudic, Christian medieval, and Reformation sources or the recent Bishops' Letter on Economic Justice; alternatively, they may examine work alienation as explored in the HEW-commissioned study, *Work in America*, and compare that with more

---

[1]*The curriculum of Educational Planning is an evolving project in which nearly all SLS faculty members take part. I am indebted to Associate Dean Ruth Mathews and Professors Clark Everling, Ana Martinez, and Steven Tischler for some of the particular approaches and activities described here.*

radical theorists such as C. Wright Mills and Erich Fromm. At the same time, students write essays on what work has meant in their own lives, what jobs they have done, and what their working lives have netted them in a sense of service, craftsmanship, pride. Work itself is defined in such a way as to include all purposeful human activity that provides a product or service to oneself or others; thus, labor that is often unpaid, such as housekeeping, artistic endeavor, and social activism, is given visibility and respect.

These initial activities seek to ground the course in both a theoretical and experiential understanding of work as a focus of human creativity and community. The course then introduces a related notion, that of work as a source of human knowledge. Students write essays about what they themselves have learned from their working lives, educational autobiographies that treat the workplace as a living classroom in which people acquire both practical and conceptual skills. Although credit awards are granted only for college-level, college-equivalent learning, faculty are careful not to make college accreditability the sole standard for what constitutes worthwhile knowledge. Studies have shown that so-called unskilled and semiskilled work requires a wide range of conceptual and problem-solving skills that are both valuable in their own right and transferrable to academic activity. Students are encouraged to make their lives as workers known to their fellow students and to articulate their sense of worth.

This is important, for these essays can be both moving and revealing of how much skill and wisdom go into what is considered semiskilled work. One student, for example, whose job as a nurse's aide in a state mental hospital puts her at the bottom of the professional ladder, had this to say about her job:

> My job is to teach people with developmental disabilities to "do for themselves." I teach them to feed themselves using forks, spoons, and plates. I teach them to drink out of a glass without spilling... There are thousands of steps and I have books which break down these tasks into the smallest movements. Buttoning a sweater might take me a year to teach someone ... Many times when I have worked with a client for many years and they get ready to leave to live in a group home, they try to be babies again. They do not want to grow up. In the end, they always leave. Once they taste freedom, they can never go back to being children. They are special adults in many ways, and will never be totally dependent again, no matter how much they are afraid of the world. They want

to grow. They do not want to return to dependence. They want to be free.

Thus, before learning to distinguish between academic versus non-academic learning, or between theoretical versus applied knowledge, students have had an opportunity to experience themselves as experts in their fields.

While all work-based knowledge may be valuable, it is not all equally empowering; there is a difference, as we point out to students, between knowing how to get from class to Central Park and learning how to read a map. The history of work, therefore, is followed by the sociology of education, by an exploration of the kinds of education available in society and the qualities of empowerment contained in each.

Classroom discussions and small group activities begin to bring out basic distinctions, such as that between procedural and conceptual knowledge or between types of education available in different types of schools. One in-class activity has been developed, for example, in which students complete two versions of a "marooned on a desert island" exercise. They are given a list of survivors, each described by name, occupation, age, height, and weight. (Information is presented in such a way that gender is not always obvious.) In the first version of the exercise, students are given a specific list of tasks and specific, rather simple-minded criteria for assigning them—"Give the two oldest people the task of cooking," "Give the two tallest people the task of picking bananas." A few trick questions are thrown in.

In this version students work alone and are publicly graded on the "test" by the instructor, who also acts as judge. In the second version students are given only the list and description of the survivors and are asked to work in small groups to identify the tasks that must be done and to assign people to those tasks using whatever criteria they choose. Once the groups are finished, they report to the class, with the instructor facilitating the discussion and pointing out the various interesting options and choices made. For homework students are asked to compare the kind of knowledge being developed through the two versions of the exercise.

Interestingly, most students return the following week to report that the first, procedural version of the exercise was the more demanding and beneficial. They praise it for inculcating those values that made for success in their own schooling: exactitude, the ability to follow directions, practice in following someone else's logic, and a sense of competition. Class discussion then brings out the skills that are developed by the second version, which often were neither taught nor valued in the schools they attended: the ability to conceptualize a situation holistically, to articulate ideas, to work with others on intellectual tasks, to make decisions.

Readings assigned at this point in the course are often used in conjunction with this and similar exercises. Students may read a variety of authors on the history and sociology of American education. Such readings include Jean Anyon's essay, "Social Class and the Hidden Curriculum of Work" or the chapters on "Tracking" and "Educational Structures" from C. H. Persell's *Education and Inequality*. At the same time students write autobiographical essays about their own schooling as children and young adults. Given our student population, these experiences all too often have been negative: tales of segregated facilities, corporal punishment, and insensitive guidance counseling abound. Still, the sharing of these essays provides for a kind of healing that is, I think, crucial for adults who have been courageous enough to try again. The internalized sense of failure is mitigated somewhat as students objectify their experience by communalizing it. The sense of outrage and frustration at past barriers can be channeled into determination for future academic success.

As with work autobiographies, these essays serve a dual purpose. Sections that discuss apprenticeship and other noncollegiate job training serve as first drafts of portfolio essays. At the same time readings and class discussion encourage students to move outward from an individual perspective and examine their own experience in the light of history, educational theory, and sociology.

Midway through, the course brings the worlds of work and school together and asks the question, what is the relationship between work organization and the proprietorship of knowledge? The central section of the course is a discussion of that relationship and of the types of knowledge and skill required of and available to various segments of the workforce.

In part, this section of the course serves as an introduction to social and economic history; students learn that what people actually do at work is determined by the history of technological innovation, demographic changes, and the organization of preindustrial and industrial societies. In some classes the presence of workers of similar job titles but different ages permits the tracing of such changes within contemporary generations; other classes include workers in such rapidly evolving industries that their own working lives are records of historical change. Still other classes present SLS faculty with a poignant question of assessment policy, the accrediting of highly developed technical skills such as hot-type printing that have become obsolete.

The School of Labor Studies offers programs on an ongoing basis to meet the needs of a particular union, employment sector, or job. Educational Planning classes are therefore offered occasionally in which all students are members of one union and in identical or similar jobs. When this is the case, this section of the course can focus on the relationship between work, knowledge, and power within a given industry. The history of an industry, the traditions of skill within job classifications, the role of new technologies and workplace organization, and the variables of race and gender within the workplace can all be examined in depth.

In one such course all students were female healthcare workers in paraprofessional jobs. These students read *Midwives, Witches and Nurses: A History of Women Healers* by Barbara Ehrenreich and Deidre English on the historical role of women in healthcare as well as sections of Ehrenreich and English's *For Her Own Good* and Paul Starr's *The Social Transformation of American Medicine* to understand the rise of institutionalized medicine and the creation of a subordinate female workforce within it.

The idea that knowledge is power plays two interconnected roles within Educational Planning classes. Because our students, like many workers, often return to school with a sense of intellectual inferiority, they need to develop a perspective on their own fears. The analysis of the division of expertise at their workplace encourages them to see what they have learned and not learned as the result of life experience, social structure, and industrial organization, not as a measure of individual intellectual ability.

This same idea, that access to knowledge is a key to power relationships, plays an equally important role in the second half of Educational Planning, which moves from prior learning assessment to the development of students' degree program plans. Just as in the development of their portfolios, the analysis of their own situation serves as the basis for helping students identify what they still need to learn. SLS students tend to be a self-selected population; they have chosen, or have been sent by their unions, to gain social scientific and preprofessional training in economic, organizational, and technological trends. Their goals tend to revolve around advocacy and organizational empowerment; even those with individual goals for their education are most often interested in careers as labor lawyers, safety and health professionals, trade union leaders, and the like. Thus, the analysis of the current workplace environment and the likely effects on workers of forthcoming changes provides a perspective on how best to use education to prepare themselves. A student in a high-tech industry such as telecommunications, for example, may identify computer literacy as an individual educational goal; but he or she may also choose to study the impact of computerization on the communications industry, the centralization and downsizing of the workforce, the globalization of corporate communications, and the safety and health ''dos'' and ''don'ts'' of operating a computer terminal.

The SLS faculty, most of whom teach Educational Planning on a regular basis, has developed a number of strategies for rooting these complex issues in students' individual experience. One such strategy is in the form of an exercise in which students are presented with a first-person narrative that gives a casual portrait of a day on the job, titled ''Every Day When I Go To Work.'' The details vary, but a class with a large number of public sector clerical workers might be given an essay similar to the following.

Hi. My name is Mary.

Every day when I go to work, I have the same routine. I work as a clerk for the Department of Housing in New York City taking down information on code violations. People call in when they have a problem. Sometimes it's noisy neighbors or drug addicts in the hallways. Sometimes they can't find the landlord to get their lights or plumbing repaired. In the winter, most of the complaints are about lack of heat or hot water.

When I first started working here, I sat by the phone, took down the information, and then made a decision about what to do. I might call the police, send an emergency repair team, contact the code violations bureau to report the landlord, whatever. I used to get headaches from the noise of all those phones ringing, and it used to drive me crazy trying to track down the right people to solve a particular problem, but between phone calls, the other women and I used to get to kid around. Now, with the new equipment they've brought in, the whole job is different. No more ringing phones—a call comes in through a red light above my computer terminal. The screen shows me the questions to ask, and as the people talk, I type in the answers. Then I sign off. Based on the answers I indicate, the computer sends the report out.

In some ways, my job is a lot easier now; at least I don't have to try to keep track of where the teams are all the time. And it's a lot quieter. Still, I feel kind of tied to that computer, and I don't have much chance to talk to my coworkers anymore. Despite the quiet, I still seem to get headaches. And I miss being able to call Sally down at the precinct or Joe on the emergency team to find out what happened about a particular complaint.

After reading this essay, students will be asked to work at home or in small groups to answer the questions, "What does Mary have to learn about in order to understand her situation at work? In order to improve it?"

The answers students typically give contain a variety of approaches. Some focus on career change or advancement: to get another job Mary should take advantage of and improve upon her preliminary computer skills, or she should study personnel management and try to move up the civil service ladder. Other approaches are trade-union oriented: Mary and her coworkers should learn better negotiating skills to bargain for improvements in the work environment, or they should study the occupational hazards of CRT usage to find out why she still gets headaches. Still other approaches point to liberal arts education: Mary needs to understand the economics of housing and public employment, the psychology of work identification and satisfaction, the impact of computers on human communications, and the structure of public and private sectors within the urban environment. The various approaches are treated as valid and interconnected, making the point that a worker's ability to understand and control his or her work environment depends on access to many kinds of knowledge—the development and retention of individual job skills, of course, but also the expertise to work effectively for collective ends and the conceptual, holistic understanding of the attending social realities.

A second strategy for helping students to think broadly about their educational needs is based on the previous discussion of the division of knowledge within the workforce. Students from the same or related industries work in small groups and are asked to list answers to the following questions: "What do the workers on my job need to know?" "What kinds of knowledge are typical of management as a whole?" Comparisons of the two lists make clear to students the different levels of empowerment produced by different kinds of knowledge. Especially those workers in rapidly changing sectors are quick to articulate the liberal arts and social science basis of the ability to anticipate and plan for the future; one group of telephone installers and repairers, for example, listed the following as areas of knowledge fundamental to the management of New York Telephone: theoretical electronics, instrumentation and measurement, corporate planning, domestic and international economics, the legal framework, finance, communication theory, prediction and goals formulation, comparative world politics, social psychology, and the interface of business and government.

Thus, both portfolio development and degree program planning take place within the broadening context of the study of work itself. The portfolios and degree programs thus produced undergo the same assessment and review procedures as others at Empire State College, but the focus of the course itself is students' introduction to the subject matter of labor studies. Classes conclude with an examination of the SLS curriculum, both the courses that make up the social science foundations and the specialized possibilities for advanced study: labor-management relations, occupational safety and health, working women's studies, union leadership, benefit fund administration, and other options that are adapted for particular students' needs.

As the above description makes clear, the structure and subject matter of Educational Planning is particular to the curriculum of SLS. Its outlines, however, have important implications for other institutions and fields. First, courses such as this serve an important function in college programs for adults in which (and this is the vast majority) a large majority of students work for a living. By making the experience of workers not simply a source of ''prior'' learning but also a field of intellectual inquiry, the course introduces students to an academic curriculum that takes seriously the realities of their lives. To their credit, labor educators have long known what many adult educators are now learning, namely, that the experiences of working people are of historical and cultural significance and that true access to higher education requires not only entrance into academic institutions but visibility within them.

Second, introductory courses that involve the study of work give working-class students a natural transition between previous experiential learning and new academic modes of thought. The inclusion of relevant subject matter alone does not guarantee success in college: labor history, labor sociology, and labor economics are still history, sociology, and economics. By making students' own experiences the first ''text'' of classroom-based academic learning, however, educators can build on students' own analytical and conceptual tools and break down the perceived isolation between students' own understanding and the world of academic thought.

Finally, labor studies serves as a model for the other interdisciplinary social sciences that are, in effect, the new humanities. In women's studies, African American studies, and similar fields, students seek to deepen their understanding of self through the broadening of perspective and the analysis of historical and social relationships. Portfolio development thus serves as a natural introduction to all of these new, interdisciplinary fields. The traditional dictum, ''Know thyself,'' takes on a concrete and immediate meaning as more nontraditional students seek to use the academy to examine their individual and collective lives.

The College of Public and Community Service of the University of Massachusetts, Boston, is similar to the Van Arsdale School of Labor Studies in the explicit relationship between its student body and the curriculum. In this case the ethnic and cultural diversity of the students is an important aspect of a curriculum based on community service in an urban environment.

As author Clark Taylor explains, the Assessment course uses issues of cultural pluralism as part of an "Introduction to a Field" approach focused on the urban environment. "One approach," Taylor explains, "is to identify learning outcomes that arise from people's experience of race, class, and culture that can be evaluated as prior learning and addressed with opportunities for new learning. A central task, then, is to pin down the implications of these factors for service delivery and for relations among service providers and managers in the workplace."

COLLEGE OF PUBLIC AND COMMUNITY SERVICE, UNIVERSITY OF MASSACHUSETTS, BOSTON

Clark Taylor

In the summer of 1972 a small group of planning faculty gathered in Boston to create the College of Public and Community Service (CPCS), a new unit of the University of Massachusetts in Boston. The challenge for the planners of this new college was to bring shape to an assigned set of innovations just at the time when protest dried up on campuses and administrators' heads were filling with thoughts of retrenchment. Undeterred, we plunged ahead.

Prior learning assessment was just one of a group of innovative elements spliced into CPCS. Planners were charged with creating a program that would be interdisciplinary and field oriented and that would integrate liberal arts and career education studies. Prior learning assessment fit in as one part of the competency-based, outcomes-oriented curriculum that resulted.

Competency-based education became the model of CPCS for a number of interrelated reasons, as part of a felt need to measure student progress and accredit learning while avoiding a focus on courses and grades. Students for the new college were to be urban adults, broadly representative of the racial, class, and cultural diversity of urban Boston. CPCS faculty would be an integrated mix of academics and practitioners drawn from the career fields of human and community service that the new program would address in its curriculum. Dominating this complex agenda was a commitment on the part of the new leadership at the campus and university levels to place CPCS on the leading edge of the university's involvement with the city of Boston.

CPCS today enrolls some 1100 students, including 70 graduate students. It is part of UMass, Boston, an urban university that incorporates a variety of innovations throughout its several campuses but that is at the same time a traditional research-oriented institution. Established as a part of the state university system only twenty-two years ago, UMass Boston has grown up in what has been called the "fallout area of HarMIT;" this has stamped a competitive mold on the enterprise, resulting in aspirations of greatness and feelings of insecurity. CPCS is one of five constituent colleges within the university's Boston campus.

As a case study of prior learning assessment, then, CPCS has a particular history, one of prior learning in a college keyed to urban activism and a public service curriculum. As such, the experience of CPCS is instructive for those committed to making the benefits of higher education and preprofessional training effectively available to everyone, including those who have been previously excluded because of race or class.

The Bachelor of Arts degree is awarded to CPCS students who complete fifty competencies in the required pattern of distribution. Competencies are the basic unit of credit at the college and are certified when students demonstrate skills and knowledge according to predetermined standards and criteria. Related competencies are grouped into certificates, and five certificates, adding up to the fifty competencies, must be completed for the degree, as follows: language, mathematics, general education, career, and independent interest.

When new students arrive at the beginning of a semester, they are automatically enrolled in the one required course of the college. Called *Assessment*, the course has several key purposes: (1) to orient new students to the CPCS curriculum, (2) to provide the understanding necessary for students to identify relevant prior experiential learning and present evidence of their competence, (3) to plan the new learning they need to complete their degree program, and (4) to serve as a source of support for students in their first semester. Assessment is cotaught by a faculty member and a continuing CPCS student who has completed a minimum of half of the competencies necessary for a degree. The faculty member serves as each student's academic advisor for the semester. The student coteacher is someone who has been through the ropes and is able to advise new students on the basis of actual experience with the program. All faculty members in the college are expected to teach Assessment at least once, and most do it from time to time. A few particularly enjoy it, are good at it, and teach it fairly regularly. Sections vary quite a bit, depending on the coteachers' style, and there is no effort to develop a uniform model.

On their first day of the course students get their assignment to a section of eighteen–twenty people and are given the Red Book, a looseleaf notebook containing the complete set of choices of competency statements, and a manual that provides a written walk-through of the CPCS program. These materials can be overwhelming. After all, here is *everything* a student will need to do to receive a degree. Fortunately, each student has an immediate opportunity to meet others in the same circumstances and to learn that there is a process at hand that they can master.

The Assessment course lasts through the whole semester. The first two weeks are intensive, with two three-hour sessions per week during which students learn how to function in this very different curricular system. Also during this period students get the results of reading and writing diagnostics taken just before the semester started and a report of competencies they will receive from transfer of prior college work. As part of getting acquainted with the Red Book, students find a competency called, "who am I/what do I plan to learn?" This is the baseline competency for the Assessment course itself. Its outcome is a learning plan, in which the student details the entire set of competencies chosen for the degree, both those to be done on the basis of prior learning and those that will involve at least some new learning. A key to the learning plan is a statement of the student's academic and career goals, and curriculum choices must be justified against the goal statement.

Starting with the third week students can begin other courses that are designed to start that week to accommodate Assessment students. Assessment continues to meet once a week, with particular focus on the tools needed to assess and present evidence for one's prior experiential learning. By midsemester the focus shifts somewhat to accommodate students' individual questions through supplementary one on one meetings with the faculty and student coteachers. Group sessions can be used as each group chooses, and many decide to include demonstration of competencies such as those in public speaking.

Assessment groups are often lively, even exciting, in the level of sharing and growth they produce. CPCS students are a diverse lot, and groups typically run the gamut of race, class, age, community, and career interests. The majority of students are women, reflected the composition of the workforce in human services, from which many CPCS students come. Ages range from the early twenties to the seventies, with the average being thirty-eight.

Students often identify their colearners as among the richest resources in the college, and we encourage them to do so—our informal slogan is "Diversity makes us great." A variety of participatory activities, including small group work and role plays, help Assessment sections develop a sense of community and connect students through an examination of one another's strengths and needs.

The vast majority of students who complete Assessment produce the learning plan, which means they have completed one of the competencies toward the degree. Most will have completed at least one or two additional competencies as part of the course, typically including a speaking competency. Some find that they can complete many more competencies based on prior learning, in some cases through consultation with faculty in other curricular areas of the college. It is important to note here that students are by no means limited to the Assessment course or their first semester for the demonstration of prior learning; because the curriculum is based on outcomes, they are encouraged to do so throughout their time at the college. Most curricular areas offer workshops that help students identify and demonstrate prior learning.

Our fifteen years of experience with assessment have shown the faculty of CPCS that prior learning and outcomes education are a natural meld. In effect, prior learning assessment always requires some form of competency-based strategy, either overt or covert; criteria and standards for evaluation are either stated or implied whenever learning from experience is assessed. The key with defined and articulated competencies is for those standards and criteria to be accessible both to faculty evaluators and to the students to be evaluated. The CPCS faculty has discovered how difficult it is to arrive at publicly stated outcomes; yet most, if not all, believe the effort has been worth the cost in terms of benefit for students.

The linking of outcomes education with urban adult students poses a host of critical questions: which outcomes, and toward what purposes? Students who come from a rich range of racial, ethnic, cultural, generational, and educational backgrounds have a great deal to learn from one another as well as from the formal curriculum. But how can the benefits arising from the mix be maximized? How can the strengths inherent in the diversity the range of backgrounds be recognized and woven into the curricular design?

CPCS has addressed the latter question, in part, by identifying some competencies that typically derive from the experiential learning of urban adults. These include "building social networks," "individual roles in groups," and "cultural awareness." The point here, of course, is to value the learning of people who have often seen themselves as outsiders to higher education.

A related problem for prior learning programs is how to deal with skill deficiencies. The task of assessing one's prior experiential learning calls for fairly sophisticated communication and analytical skills. Does this mean that only those entering college with such skills should be considered for credit from prior learning? Of course not. CPCS has used a number of strategies to address this problem. One was a program called Intensive Assessment, a year-long course that involved intensive work on reading and writing skills combined with assessment of one or more of the competencies named in the paragraph above. Variations on this approach are currently under consideration.

A commitment to making prior learning evaluation work for the poor, for working-class people, for people of color, and for students drawn from various ethnic backgrounds has further implications. High on the list is the need to surface issues of race, class, and culture and to address them directly. One approach is to identify learning outcomes that arise from people's experience of race, class, and culture. These outcomes can be evaluated as prior learning for students who already meet them; at the same time they can form a basis for curriculum development and be addressed with opportunities for new learning.

Two competency statements at CPCS are relevant here. The first, "cultural awareness," is a part of the general education curriculum and calls for students to use cultural theory to identify aspects of their own culture and to compare their cultural experiences with that of at least two other cultures. The other is "race and culture in human services," which directs students to identify variant characteristics between the dominant racial and cultural group and two racial and cultural subgroups. This serves as a foundation for identifying both individual and institutional aspects of discrimination based on racial and cultural factors. A central task, then, is to pin down the implications of these factors for service delivery and for relations among service providers and managers in the workplace.

The suggestion above, to define race, class, and cultural outcomes as a basis for prior learning evaluation, is meant to be illustrative only. If assessment of prior learning is to transcend these profound barriers to meaning and opportunity, attention to these factors will have to become pervasive. My point here is not to suggest that race, culture, and class issues should be the entire curriculum. It is, rather, that these crucial factors should get the full attention they deserve in the evaluation of prior learning, as well as in all other areas of the institution.

A final implication for prior learning programs intended for the full range of potential students is that affirmative action must become affirmative reality. Though committed from its beginning to a diverse racial and cultural mix of students, faculty, and staff, CPCS was in fact a white-dominated college during its early years. More recently a black dean has successfully recruited additional faculty and staff of color, triggering a reassessment of our commitments and practice. This change has created confusion and pain for some, but it is the basis for healthy growth in an area that vitally affects assessment of prior learning for previously marginalized students.

CPCS has by no means a definitive model for addressing the above issues. But the commitments and experience of this young college raise these issues in ways that may be helpful to others. The college is committed to serving diversely prepared adult urban students, including a substantial proportion of people of color. As a College of Public and Community Service, we are committed as well to an activist stance on issues that affect urban students. Our program of prior learning assessment attempts to respond to the strengths as well as the needs of our culturally rich student population. Some outcome statements are defined to affirm the kind of learning urban adult students often develop in their home, community, and work experience. Students can be evaluated for prior learning throughout their program at the college, which both takes pressure off the first semester and allows time for the development of skills necessary to the analysis and articulation of prior learning. A feature of the assessment program, described above, is that continuing students, who have already had some of their experiential learning evaluated, serve as coinstructors to assist new students with that phase of their program.

Finally, issues of race, class, and culture are addressed directly in the curriculum. They form a basis both for the assessment of prior learning and for rich new learning in CPCS's diverse student population. The college's experience underscores the fact that prior learning assessment is loaded with racial, class, and cultural, as well as educational, implications. These factors cannot be ignored if the prior learning movement is to be part of the answer to the problems of higher education in a complex world.

Because of the college's commitment to individualized instruction, many Empire State College students design highly individualized degree programs and complete their prior learning assessment through individual tutorials. In this final essay, Alan Mandell provides one example of this individualized "Degree Design" approach. "Here," says the author, "is a good opportunity for the student to participate not only in the design of an academic program but of the degree program planning 'course.'"

EMPIRE STATE COLLEGE, STATE UNIVERSITY OF NEW YORK (B)

Alan Mandell

Empire State College was founded in 1971 as the alternative institution within the State University of New York for adult higher education. As a college, it is dedicated to individualized education and centered on a tutorial system where faculty mentors and students work together to develop specific learning components and whole degree programs that are responsive to students' needs. Thus, the designing for each student of an individualized plan of study is both the most cherished educational ideal of Empire State College and its primary delivery mode.

Because of the individualized nature of degree program planning, the college structure for program approval and the assessment of prior learning is organized first around student–faculty interaction and second around a careful series of faculty and administrative reviews. Small interdisciplinary faculty review committees meet in regional centers throughout the state to discuss and judge student portfolios, and a further all-college evaluation takes place in the college's administrative headquarters in Saratoga Springs.

A student's work on prior learning assessment and curricular decision making takes place through participation in Degree Program Planning, typically a four-credit study in portfolio development and degree design described, as are all individualized studies, in a detailed "learning contract." The college offers a variety of group approaches to these activities (see, for example, essays by Elana Michelson and by Jane Shipton and Elizabeth Steltenpohl in this volume). Most students, however, carry out their assessment and planning activities through individual work with a faculty member. It is this one-to-one approach to assessment and degree program planning that is the subject of this essay.

The tailoring of the planning process to the individual's academic background and personal and professional interests means that many of the activities that make up the portfolio development "course" itself cannot be named before the actual work with a student begins. In effect, the student is encouraged to participate in the designing not only of his or her undergraduate program but of the portfolio planning study itself. The crafting of this central learning component in a student's life at Empire State College serves many purposes, not least of which is providing an important occasion for the faculty mentor to listen: to learn about a student's interests, strengths, and limitations and to help the student articulate significant personal and professional goals that can ultimately gain expression within the academic plan. When the learning contract is successful, this planning process is a truly collaborative effort in which conversation, ongoing guidance from the faculty member, and the active participation of the student all contribute to the completion of a degree program plan.

No one student, of course, and no one individualized degree program plan can begin to articulate the range of options that mentors can turn to in their planning work with students. The example presented here, however, seeks to bring to light a *process* of thinking, working, and experimenting that is central to individualized assessment and program planning. Indeed, the student discussed here may not be typical—he is younger and has fewer family and work responsibilities, for example, than many of our students. But his experience accentuates the necessary engagement in a series of issues and concerns and the structured, yet at times improvisational, nature of helping an individual student develop a meaningful academic plan.

Michael came to Empire State College having completed more than eighty credits at another university. Although he was relatively young by the college's standards, his experiences in college had already helped him to think about the kinds of studies that interested him. He was also sensitive to the ways of studying he had found difficult and was quick to analyze the reasons for his previous college failures. Before any concrete plan of work was formalized, we spent a number of tutorial sessions talking quite generally about his plans and interests and about the workings of Empire State College. These were often rather unfocused discussions; perhaps they even served as hours for each of us to listen, to pick up hints of opportunities, and to feel each other out with the full knowledge that a formal learning contract would have to be developed from these discussions. In many ways, Michael's habits of reflection and self-scrutiny and his seeming comfort in questioning his ideas and motives made the beginnings of this planning process less alien to him than it may have been to another kind of student. He was surely one of those students for whom analyzing and wondering and questioning served as a regular quality of everyday life that he wanted to transfer to this planning process.

Michael came into these sessions with many interesting though amorphous ideas about future plans, with criticisms of his previous educational experiences, and with only a minimal sense of what he might do to get from his present thoughts to the creation of a degree program plan. He spoke of his abiding fascination with nature, his high school practicum on a working farm, and his current employment in the field of carpentry. He knew that all of these experiences fit together in some way, and hoped that together we could find a thread, a theme, around which to design his undergraduate "major." He was very aware of Empire State as a place where he could pursue this kind of individualized academic search, although in the early weeks I wondered whether his excitement over curricular flexibility somewhat hid his own ambivalence about taking responsibility for his studies.

After our second session I realized that, although we both genuinely enjoyed out time together, Michael needed specific impetus for more systematic reflection. He had begun to understand (and use) the language of Empire State College and could describe the kinds of expectations that he had to consider in his own degree. But while he continually voiced real interest in defining his own curriculum, he was making little progress in doing so. He knew that I was intrigued by his academic and life concerns—I had said as much quite directly—but I wanted to find a way for him to take the next steps on his own. I thus suggested that we each come to the next session with a list of books and articles and authors that reflected our independent understandings of Michael's interests. This step, I thought, might help Michael to name what was important to him more carefully and to integrate his ideas and those of a selected group of authors in a specific way.

Our third session was spent comparing notes. We each had brought in our separate lists and were both excited to find texts and authors in common. I was surprised to find authors on my list whose ideas he was unfamiliar with, and he was quick to describe books on carpentry and home design that made important connections between ecology and everyday life that were far from my own way of thinking. Together we decided on a list of readings. As the learning contract came to state, "The goal in this part of his study is to search for different vocabularies that can help [Michael] express his own desires and interests." There were nine texts listed, including works by E.F. Schumacher and Theodore Roszak, poems by Gary Snyder, essays by John Dewey and Buckminster Fuller, and a recent biography of John Muir. We decided together that a mixture of theoretical work and the materials dealing with practical issues, with ideas and people of the past, and with contemporary social critics would provide the kind of variety we wanted. Over the the course of the next few meetings some of the titles were changed as we both located new materials, but we had found a way to develop a context, a foundation for Michael's own degree studies.

Once the learning contract for Michael's Degree Program Planning was formalized, we met biweekly to discuss the books and writings. We decided that Michael would keep a journal of ideas, responses, and points of interest that would also include issues and topics that he found he knew little about. At our tutorial sessions we used this quite informal log as a take-off point for our discussion about "human–earth relations," the phrase that for Michael began to sum up his point of focus. What was important was that Michael was finding out about other ideas and perspectives, including the theoretical debates in the area, which allowed him to began to see his own perspective in context. Comparing and contrasting, asking questions about his own assumptions, and critically evaluating ideas that were distinct from his own were a regular part of our meetings.

At the same time Michael decided to do another kind of searching. He investigated other college curricula in various areas, such as environmental studies, ecology, social ecology, and environmental design. He also wrote to and received information from specialized programs, such as the New Alchemy Institute in Woods Hole, Massachusetts. Many of our most interesting discussions focused on these different vocabularies, on the sometimes subtle differences between a program that focused on the natural sciences, one that depended on sociocultural studies for its core, and others that were more truly interdisciplinary. Michael spoke to professors in local departments and teachers from his past who could offer their own perspective on his efforts to name a focus of study and develop a plan of study that would be personally challenging and academically strong.

It was also in the context of his developing plans for future study that the assessment of Michael's prior learning took place. As mentioned above, Michael had a number of years of good experience in the world of carpentry. He had read many books and articles on home design, developed significant standards of craftsmanship, and worked with any number of carpenters whose design and quality of work had reflected Michael's own concerns with ecological principles. Here obviously was an area where Michael might gain credit for prior experiential learning.

Prior learning at Empire State College is not evaluated on either a course-equivalent or a competency-based model; rather, students must establish that they have significant learning in a particular area, that their learning meets the standards of college-level and college-accreditable knowledge, and that their learning makes a meaningful contribution to their overall degree design. Michael was thus expected to write an essay in which he described his experience and knowledge of carpentry and home design that would focus on what he had done and read, what he had learned from these varied activities, and why this knowledge was important to him. Michael developed a number of drafts that we discussed and then met with a professional in the field to have this experience evaluated. Through this process, Michael was able to include in his final degree program plan an area that he had not studied in formal college course work but that was extremely pertinent to his understanding of "human–earth relations."

As in most colleges, transcript credits from accredited colleges and universities are easier to include in an Empire State College degree than less formal forms of learning; nonetheless, we also spent many hours reflecting on Michael's transcript studies. Could he begin to think about the links between what he knew and had studied and what he did not know and needed to study? Here again our discussions of his previous college transcript served as the occasion for a process of reflection that not only encouraged Michael to think about his past college experiences but to continue to think about the academic areas that he wanted to integrate in his Empire State degree. Thus, for example, our discussion about the differences between the environmental design courses and those of the biology department that focused on ecology helped Michael become more attentive to the assumptions of certain fields and particular thinkers and to the need to help others understand why he pursued the direction that he had chosen. Empire State requires that an essay of exploration and explanation accompany each student's degree plan; having to explain to others why a particular study has been chosen adds additional perspective and awareness to the overall planning process.

This was not an easy process, nor one that followed the kind of linear, rational route that might be communicated through this description. The parts of Michael's Degree Program Planning contract, which he himself named reflection, investigation, reading, and synthesis, did not always flow easily. There were meetings where I wondered to myself whether Michael's desire to craft such an individualized and interdisciplinary degree was beyond his present capabilities. There were other moments when I wondered if Michael wanted to develop a degree that excluded areas that were more alien to him, such as biology, zoology, and geography. And there were other meetings where, having drawn up a list of possible studies to be included in his degree, I wondered if he had established academically sound criteria to determine what would and would not be included in his final program plan.

These kinds of questions were complex, impossible to answer easily, always changing, and probably an inevitable outgrowth of this kind of open-ended and personal process of reflection. I truly wanted to be a guide in this project, although I felt an equal responsibility to communicate my own criteria for a meaningful undergraduate program and those of Empire State College as well. This was an abiding tension throughout our months of work on the program, a tension we discussed on any number of occasions. I also knew, as did Michael, that his degree program would have to be reviewed by an academic committee from across the disciplines and again by an administrative office. This structure of program review gave me some necessary distance and also encouraged Michael to understand that it was not *my* evaluation that would determine the acceptance of his final program. He had to create an individual curriculum that others, not only the single person with whom he had been talking, could understand. In addition to using our own college review structure, I continued to use as a point of reference in our talks some anonymous department chair in ecology or environmental studies who might not agree with every choice Michael made, but who would be able to recognize the perspectives as those most central to this complex field of inquiry.

In the end, Michael's synthesis was surely his own, one that emphasized the areas of learning that excited him the most. But it also included new studies, one in botany and another in geology, for example, that reflected his growing awareness of different ideas and the degree expectations of other institutions. Michael was able to attain his goal; he had developed an undergraduate curriculum based on his own interests and priorities, on informed decisions regarding other program models, and on the ideas and directions of professionals in related fields. But while a concrete plan was a tangible and important outcome of this project, perhaps even more significant for Michael was his serious engagement in a process of reflection. Michael had communicated his own ideas and visceral responses to ways of living, wondered about the ramifications of different attitudes and social practices, and explored the myriad ways in which one can approach a task of intellectual inquiry. Perhaps it is these aspects of planning an individualized degree program that Michael will remember, and that will offer him guidance as he continues to study and to work in his chosen field.

BIBLIOGRAPHY

The following citations are clustered around general concerns introduced in this book. Many of the texts are intended to provide background information for instructors of portfolio development courses. Other books and essays can be used by students as reference works in a specific area of interest. The selection is not definitive.

The Theory and Practice of Prior Learning Assessment

Dewees, Patricia. *The Assessment of Prior Learning: A Critical Adult Learner Service*. Athens, Ohio: Project Learn, 1986.

Ekstrom, Ruth B., Abigail M. Harris, and Marlaine E. Lockheed. *How to Get College Credit for What You Have Learned as a Home-Maker and Volunteer*. Princeton: Educational Testing Service, 1977.

Keeton, Morris T. *Experiential Learning: Rationale, Characteristics, and Assessment*. San Francisco: Jossey-Bass, 1976.

Keeton, Morris T., and Pamela J. Tate, eds. *Learning by Experience— What, Why, How*. San Francisco: Jossey-Bass, 1978.

Knapp, Joan. *Assessing Prior Learning*. Columbia, Md.: CAEL, 1977.

Kolb, David A. *Experiential Learning: Experience as the Source of Learning and Development*. Englewood Cliffs, N. J.: Prentice-Hall, 1984.

Moon, Rexford G., and Gene R. Hawes, eds. *Developing New Adult Clienteles by Recognizing Prior Learning*. San Francisco: Jossey-Bass, 1981.

Schlossberg, Nancy K., Ann Q. Lynch, and Arthurn Chickering. *Improving Higher Education Environments for Adults*. San Francisco: Jossey-Bass, 1989.

Simosko, Susan. *Earn College Credit for What You Know*. Washington, D.C.: Acropolis, 1985.

Simosko, Susan, and associates. *Assessing Learning: A CAEL Handbook for Faculty*. Columbia, Md.: CAEL, 1988.

Warren, Jonathan, and Paul Breen. *The Educational Value of Portfolio and Learning Contract Development*. Columbia, Md.: CAEL, 1981.

Whittaker, Urban. *Assessing Learning: Standards, Principles and Procedures*. Philadelphia: CAEL, 1989.

Adult Development and Lifelong Learning

Aslanian, Carol B., and H.B. Brickell. *Americans in Transition: Life Changes as Reasons for Adult Learning*. Princeton: College Board, 1980.

Belenky, Mary F., et al. *Women's Ways of Knowing: The Development of Self, Voice and Mind*. New York: Basic Books, 1986.

Brookfield, Stephen D. *Understanding and Facilitating Adult Learning: A Comprehensive Analysis of Principles and Effective Practices*. San Francisco: Jossey-Bass, 1986.

Cross, K. Patricia. *Adults as Learners: Increasing Participation and Facilitating Learning*. San Francisco: Jossey-Bass, 1981.

Evans, Nancy, ed. *Facilitating the Development of Women*. San Francisco: Jossey-Bass, 1985.

Evans, Norman. *Post-Education Society: Recognizing Adults as Learners*. London: Croom Helm, 1985.

Gilligan, Carol. *In a Different Voice: Psychological Theory and Women's Development*. Cambridge: Harvard University Press, 1982.

Gilligan, Carol, et al., eds. *Mapping the Moral Domain: A Contribution of Women's Thinking to Psychological Theory and Education*. Cambridge: Harvard University Press, 1988.

Gould, Roger L. *Transformations: Growth and Change in Adult Life*. New York: Simon and Schuster, 1978.

Gross, Ronald, ed. *Invitation to Lifelong Learning*. Chicago: Follett, 1982.

Houle, Cyril O. *An Inquiring Mind: A Study of Adults Who Continue to Learn*. Madison: University of Wisconsin Press, 1961.

Kegan, Robert. *The Evolving Self: Problem and Process in Human Development*. Cambridge: Harvard University Press, 1982.

Knowles, Malcolm. *The Adult Learner: A Neglected Species*, 3d ed. Houston: Gulf Publications, 1984.

_____. *Self-Directed Learning: A Guide for Learners and Teachers*. New York: Cambridge, 1975.

Kohlberg, Lawrence. "Stage and Sequence: The Cognitive-Developmental Approach to Socialization," in *Handbook on Socialization Theory and Research*, edited by D. A. Goslin. Chicago: Rand McNally, 1969.

Levinson, Daniel J., et al. *The Seasons of a Man's Life*. New York: Knopf, 1978.

Menson, Betty, ed. *Building on Experiences in Adult Development: New Directions in Experiential Learning #16*. San Francisco: Jossey-Bass, 1982.

Merriam, Sharan B. *Selected Writings on the Philosophy of Adult Education*. Melbourne, Fla.: Kriefer, 1984.

Mezirow, Jack. "A Critical Theory of Adult Learning and Education." *Adult Education* 32, no. 1 (Fall, 1981).

_____. "Perspective Transformation." *Studies in Adult Education* 9, no. 2 (1977).

Neugarten, Bernice L. *Middle Age and Aging*. Chicago: University of Chicago Press, 1968.

Schlossberg, Nancy K. *Counseling Adults in Transition*. New York: Springer, 1984.

Sheehy, Gail. *Passages: Predictable Crises of Adult Life*. New York: Dutton, 1976.

Wlodkowski, Raymond J. *Enhancing Adult Motivation to Learn*. San Francisco: Jossey-Bass, 1985.

Academic Skills and College Orientation

Barzun, Jacques, and Henry Graff. *The Modern Researcher*. 4th ed. New York: Harcourt, Brace, and Janovich, 1985.

Beasley, David. *How to Use a Research Library*. New York: Oxford University Press, 1988.

Brookfield, Stephen. *Developing Critical Thinkers: Challenging Adults to Explore Alternative Ways of Thinking and Acting*. San Francisco: Jossey-Bass, 1987.

Buerk, Dorothy. "The Voices of Women Making Meaning in Mathematics." *Journal of Education* 167, no. 3 (1985).

Elbow, Peter. *Writing without Teachers*. New York: Oxford University Press, 1973.

Haponski, William C., and Charles E. McCabe. *Back to School—The College Guide for Adults*. Princeton: Peterson's Guides, 1982.

Hecht, Miriam, and Lillian Traub. *Dropping Back In: How to Complete Your College Education Quickly and Economically*. New York: Dutton, 1982.

Horwitz, Lucy, and Lou Ferleger. *Statistics for Social Change*. Boston: South End Press, 1980.

Kolb, David A. *The Learning Styles Inventory: Technical Manual*. Boston: McBer, 1976.

Lakein, Alan. *How to Get Control of Your Time and Your Life*. New York: New American Library, 1974.

Lawrence, Betty Hurley. *Getting to Know You: Discovering Mathematics—A Guide for the Math-Avoidant Adult*. Saratoga Springs, NY: Empire State College, 1988.

Mann, Thomas. *A Guide to Library Research Methods*. 2d ed. New York: Oxford University Press, 1987.

Mendelsohn, Pam. *Happier by Degrees: A College Reentry Guide for Women*. rev. ed. Berkeley: Ten Speed Press, 1986.

Meyers, Chet. *Teaching Students to Think Critically*. San Francisco: Jossey-Bass, 1986.

Mezirow, Jack. *Fostering Critical Reflection in Adulthood: A Guide to Transformative and Emancipatory Learning*. San Francisco: Joseey-Bass, 1990.

Pauk, Walter. *How to Study in College*. 3d ed. Boston: Houghton-Mifflin, 1984.

Rivers, William, and Susan L. Harrington. *Finding Facts: Research Writing across the Curriculum*. 2d ed. Englewood Cliffs, N.J.: Prentice-Hall, 1988.

Rose, Mike. "The Language of Exclusion: Writing Instruction at the University." *College English* 47 (April, 1985).

Roszak, Theodore. *The Cult of Information: the Folklore of Computers and the True Art of Thinking*. New York: Pantheon, 1986.

Ryan, Monnie. *Whatcha Gonna Be When You Grow Up? A Guide for the Older Woman Who Wants to Go to College*. Niles, Ohio: 1978.

Shaughnessy, Mina P. *Errors and Expectations: A Guide for the Teacher of Basic Writing*. New York: Oxford Universtiy Press, 1977.

Siebert, Al and Bernadine Gilpin. *Time for College: When You Work, Have a Family, and Want More From Life*. Portland, Oregon: Practical Psychology Press, 1989.

Smith, Robert M. *Learning How to Learn: Applied Theory for Adults*. New York: Cambridge Books, 1982.

Tobias, Sheila. *Overcoming Math Anxiety*. New York: Houghton-Mifflin, 1980.

Whitaker, Urban, and Paul Breen. *Bridging the Gap: A Learner's Guide to Transferable Skills*. San Francisco: Learning Center, 1983.

Self-Assessment and Goal Searching

Berman, Eleanor. *Re-Entering: Successful Back-to-Work Strategies for Women Seeking a Fresh Start*. New York: Crown, 1980.

Bolles, Richard N. *The Three Boxes of Life (And How to Get Out of Them)*. Berkeley: Ten Speed Press, 1978.

_____. *What Color Is Your Parachute? A Practical Manual for Job Hunters and Career Changes*. Berkeley: Ten Speed Press, 1983.

Bourque, Susan C., and Donna Divine, eds. *Women Living Change*. Philadelphia: Temple University Press, 1985.

Brown, Duane, et al., eds. *Career Choice and Development*. San Francisco: Jossey-Bass, 1985.

Das, Ram, and Paul Gorman. *How Can I Help?: Stories and Reflections on Service*. New York: Knopf, 1985.

Ford, G. A., and G. L. Lippitt. *Planning Your Future: A Workbook for Personal Goal Setting*. San Diego: University Associates, 1976.

Gornick, Vivian. *Women in Science: Portraits of a World in Transition*. New York: Simon & Schuster, 1983.

Gysbers, Norman, and Earl Moore. *Career Counselling: Skills and Techniques for Practitioners*. Englewood Cliffs, N.J.: Prentice-Hall, 1987.

Haldane, Bernard. *Career Satisfaction and Success: How to Know and Manage Your Strengths*. Rev. ed. New York: American Management Association, 1982.

Haponski, William, and Charles McCabe. *New Horizons: The Education and Career Planning Guide for Adults*. Princeton: Peterson Guides, 1985.

Holland, John. *The Self-Directed Search: A Guide to Educational and Vocational Planning*. Odessa, Fla.: Psychological Assessment Resources, 1970.

Howe, Florence, ed. *Women and the Power to Change*. New York: McGraw-Hill, 1975.

Kingston, Maxine Hong. *The Woman Warrior.* New York: Random House, 1977.

Lewis, Hunter. *A Question of Values.* New York: Harper & Row, 1990.

Malcolm X. *The Autobiography of Malcolm X.* New York: Ballantine, 1977.

Moon, William Least Heat. *Blue Highways: A Journey into America.* Boston: Little, Brown, 1982.

Rainer, Tristine. *The New Diary.* Los Angeles: Tarcher, 1978.

Roszak, Theodore. *Person/Planet.* Garden City, N.Y.: Anchor, 1978.

Russell, Anne L. *Career and Conflict: A Woman's Guide to Making Life Choices.* Englewood Cliffs, N.J.: Prentice Hall, 1982.

Sher, Barbara. *Wishcraft: How to Get What You Really Want.* New York: Ballantine, 1983.

Stone, Elizabeth. *Black Sheep & Kissing Cousins: How our Family Stories Shape Us.* New York: Times Books, 1988.

Super, Donald. "A Life-Span, Life-Space Approach to Career Development." *Journal of Vocational Behavior,* 16 (1980).

Tough, Allen. *Intentional Changes: A Fresh Approach to Helping People Change.* Chicago: Follett, 1982.

The Meaning of Education

Adams, Frank. *Unearthing the Seeds of Fire: The Idea of Highlander.* Winston-Salem, North Carolina: Blair, 1975.

Altbach, Philip, et al., eds. *Excellence in Education.* Buffalo: Prometheus, 1985.

Bowers, C.A. *Elements of a Post-Liberal Theory of Education.* New York: Teachers College Press, 1987.

Bowles, Samuel and Herbert Gintis. *Schooling in Capitalist America.* New York: Basic Books, 1976.

Chapman, Anne, ed. *Feminist Resources for Schools and Colleges: A Guide to Curricular Materials.* 3d ed. New York: Feminist Press, 1986.

Chickering, Arthur W., and associates. *The Modern American College: Responding to the New Realities of Diverse Students and a Changing Society.* San Francisco: Jossey-Bass, 1981.

Dewey, John. *Democracy and Education.* New York: Free Press, 1966.

_____. *Experience and Education*. Magnolia, Ma., Peter Smith, 1983.

Freire, Paulo. *Education for Critical Consciousness*. New York: Continuum, 1973.

Grant, Gerald. *The World We Created at Hamilton High*. Cambridge: Harvard University Press, 1988.

Grant, Nigel. *Soviet Education*. 4th ed. New York: Penguin, 1979.

Greene, Maxine. *The Dialectic of Freedom*. New York: Teachers College Press, 1988.

Gross, Beatrice and Ronald, eds. *The Great School Debate: Which Way for American Education?* New York: Simon and Schuster, 1985.

Hirsch, E.D. *Cultural Literacy: What Every American Needs to Know*. New York: Houghton-Mifflin, 1987.

Ignas, Edward, and Raymond Corsini, eds. *Comparative Educational Systems*. Englewood, Co.: Peacock, 1981.

Illich, Ivan. *De-Schooling Society*. New York: Harper and Row, 1970.

Kohl, Herbert. *Growing Minds: On Becoming a Teacher*. New York: Harper and Row, 1984.

Kozol, Jonathan. *Illiterate America*. New York: New American Library, 1986.

Littleton, Taylor, ed. *The Rights of Memory: Essays on History, Science, and American Culture*. Tuscaloosa, Ala.: University of Alabama Press, 1986.

Nasaw, David. *Schooled to Order: A Social History of Public Schooling in the United States*. New York: Oxford University Press, 1979.

Natkins, Lucille. *Our Last Term: A Teacher's Diary*. Lanham, Md.: University Press of America, 1986.

Persell, C. H. *Education and Inequality*. New York: Free Press, 1979.

"The Politics of Liberal Education." *South Atlantic Quarterly*: Vol. 89, no. 1, Winter, 1990.

Postman, Neil. *Teaching as a Conserving Activity*. New York: Delacorte, 1979.

Rodriguez, Richard. *Hunger of Memory: The Education of Richard Rodriguez*. New York: Bantam Books, 1984.

Rohlen, Thomas R. *Japan's High Schools*. Berkeley: University of California Press, 1983.

Rose, Mike. *Lives on the Boundary*. New York: Penguin, 1989.

Shor, Ira. *Critical Teaching and Everyday Life*. Boston: South End Press, 1980.

Simonson, Rick, and Scott Walker, eds. *Multi-Cultural Literacy*. St. Paul, MN.: Graywolf Press, 1988.

Spring, Joel. *A Primer of Libertarian Education*. Toronto: Black Rose, 1975.

Wigginton, Eliot. *Sometimes a Shining Moment: The Foxfire Experience—Twenty Years in a High School Classroom*. Garden City, N.Y.: Anchor, 1986.

Willis, Paul. *Learning to Labor*. New York: Columbia University Press, 1981.

The Experience of Work

Baxandall, Rosalyn, et al. *America's Working Women: A Documentary History*. New York: Vintage, 1976.

Bluestone, Barry, and Bennett Harrison. *The Deindustrialization of America*. New York: Basic Books, 1982.

Edwards, Richard. *Contested Terrain: The Transformation of the Workplace in the Twentieth Century*. New York: Basic Books, 1979.

Garson, Barbara. *The Electronic Sweatshop: How Computers Are Transforming the Office of the Future into the Factory of the Past*. New York: Simon and Schuster, 1988.

Gutman, Herbert. *Work, Culture and Society in Industrializing America: Essays in American Working-Class and Social History*. New York: Knopf, 1976.

Hirschorn, Larry. *Beyond Mechanization: Work and Technology in a Post-Industrial Age*. Cambridge: MIT Press, 1986.

———. *The Workplace Within: Psychodynamics of Organizational Life*. Cambridge: MIT Press, 1988.

Howard, Robert. *Brave New Workplace*. New York: Penguin, 1985.

Howe, Louise. *Pink Collar Workers: Inside the World of Women's Work*. New York: Avon, 1978.

Kanter, Rosabeth Moss, and Ellen Goodman. *Current Issues in Higher Education. The Changing Shape of Work: Psychological Trends in America*. Washington, D.C.: American Association for Higher Education, 1978.

Kanter, Rosabeth Moss, and Barry Stein, eds. *Life in Organizations: Workplaces as People Experience Them*. New York: Basic Books, 1979.

Kennedy, Donald, Charles Craypo, and Mary Lehman. *Labor and Technology*. University Park: Pennsylvania State University, 1982.

Kessler-Harris, Alice. *Women Have Always Worked: A Historical Overview*. New York: The Feminist Press, 1981.

Leiss, William. *Under Technology's Thumb*. Montreal: McGill-Queens University Press, 1990.

Oakley, Ann. *Woman's Work: The Housewife, Past and Present*. New York: Vintage Books, 1974.

Ollman, Bertell. *Alienation*. 2nd ed. New York: Cambridge University Press, 1977.

Shaiken, Harley. *Work Transformed: Automation and Labor in the Computer Age*. New York: Holt, Rinehart and Winston, 1984.

Terkel, Studs. *Working*. New York: Avon Books, 1975.

Work in America. Report of a Special Task Force to the Secretary of Health, Education and Welfare. Cambridge: MIT Press, 1973.

Zuboff, Shoshana. *In the Age of the Smart Machine: The Future of Work and Power*. New York: Basic Books, 1988.

NOTES ON CONTRIBUTORS

Alan Mandell is Associate Dean of the Hudson Valley Regional Learning Center of Empire State College, where he has served as a mentor in the social sciences for fifteen years. He has a Ph.D. in Sociology from City University of New York. He is editor of KAIROS, a journal of social and cultural criticism.

Elana Michelson has been a faculty member at Empire State College in New York since 1981, teaching at the Van Arsdale School of Labor Studies, and is currently Chair of the Master of Arts program in Culture and Policy Studies. She serves as a consultant for labor-management education programs. She holds a Ph.D. in English Literature from Columbia University.

Susanne Boyd has been the Coordinator of the Experiential Learning Program at Ohio University since 1980 and is the author of several texts in use in the program. She holds Master's degrees in Student Personnel from Columbia University and in Cultural Anthropology from Indiana University, where she is currently completing her Ph.D.

Muriel Dance is currently Senior Fellow at the Graduate School of Education of the Hebrew University in Jerusalem. She served as Director of Academic Advisement, Chair of Humanities, and Associate Dean of the School of New Resources, College of New Rochelle from 1977 to 1987.

Bernardin Deutsch is Professor of Psychology at Alverno College, where she has been a faculty member since 1961. She has taught Alverno's Integrated Learning Seminar for transfer students on many occasions and is the coordinator of this program.

Mary Kay Kramp is Assistant Professor of Humanities at Alverno College. She has taught the Integrated learning Seminar for transfer students since 1979.

Gail A. Hall is Associate Director of the University Without Walls of the University of Massachusetts and has worked with the program since its early days. She holds a Masters of Fine Arts in Writing and Literature from UMass and has published poetry and criticism.

Leah Harvey has been at Metropolitan State University, St Paul, Minnesota, since 1974, first as a faculty member and currrently as Dean of Curriculum. In addition, she serves nationally as a consultant in adult education. Her master's and doctoral degrees are in the field of Statistics.

Brenda Krueger directed the Credit for Lifelong Learning Program at Sinclair Community College, Dayton, Ohio, from 1978 to 1987. In addition, she directed that college's Cooperative Education Program and served on the faculty in the fields of Management, Marketing, and Communications. Currently, she is a member of the faculty of the University of Cincinnati's Division of Professional Practice. She serves as a consultant to colleges and universities, corporations, and government.

Betta LoSardo holds an AB in Philosophy from Boston College and an AM in Italian Literature from Middlebury College. Since 1980, she has been teaching courses in Italian Studies and in Assessment at DePaul University's School for New Learning in Chicago Illinois.

Robert H. McKenzie is an associate professor and Coordinator of Prior Learning Assessment in the External Degree Program of the University of Alabama. He is currently also an Associate of the Kettering Foundation, working with the application of analytical reflection to community development and public leadership.

James L. Roth is Associate Professor of History and head of the Divison of Arts and Humanities at Alverno College, where he has taught since 1976. He has been a guest lecturer and served as an external assessor in Alverno's Integrated Learning Seminar on many occasions.

Richard Roughton has been Executive Director of The Office of Continuing Studies of The American University since 1987, having previously served as Associate Professor of History and Director of Special Programs in the College of Continuing Education. In addition, he has published in his academic field of Middle Eastern History and in the field of experiential education and made frequent presentations at regional and national conferences.

Jane Shipton has served as a mentor at the Long Island Regional Learning Center of Empire State College for seven years. She works closely with students both on self-assessment and the assessment of prior learning.

Elizabeth Steltenpohl has been a mentor in Educational Studies at the Long Island Regional Learning Center of Empire State College for the past sixteen years. Her recent focus has been in applying her background in teacher education to the development of educational planning skills by students.

Dee Steffans served as Coordinator of Assessment Services for the Office of External Programs of the Vermont State Colleges from 1985 to 1988. She currently is serving as Coordinator of Instruction and Advisement for Community College of Vermont.

Clark Taylor was a founding faculty member at the College of Public and Community Service of the University of Massechussets, Boston and currently serves as an Associate Professor at the College, teaching Central American studies.